I0005417

Transitioning Embedded Systems to Intelligent Environments

by

Dr. Satwant Kaur
First Lady of Emerging Technologies®

Copyright © 2010 by Satwant Kaur

All rights reserved. This book or any portion thereof may not be reproduced or used in any manner whatsoever without the express written permission of the publisher except for the use of brief quotations in a book review.

Printed in the United States of America
First Printing, 2013

www.SatwantKaur.com

DISCLAIMER

Dr. Satwant Kaur, *First Lady of Emerging Technologies®*, expresses her own personal views and opinions in all communications including all electronic, broadcast, and print media formats. Dr. Satwant Kaur is not endorsed by any third-party affiliation, organization, or employer and all opinions are solely of Dr. Kaur's, and do not reflect the opinions and/or views of any third-party affiliation, organization, or employer. For further information, please refer to her web site www.satwantkaur.com. Dr. Satwant Kaur may be contacted at her email Satwant@DrSatwantKaur.com.

DEDICATION

To my beloved father, the most brilliant technologist
He taught me to build technologies while other girls my age were playing with dolls.

REVIEWER COMMENTS

In Intelligent Environments, countless connected embedded devices become the intelligence to connect us with all things in our environment, whether it is at home, in cars, in hospitals, at the bottom of our oceans, in our forests, or in our own clothes. We will soon be connected everywhere we go. This book details the enabling technologies and challenges, and presents a roadmap for how to get there

"Satwant lays out both a vision and data on the key technologies for the future of the embedded world. She has moved from Gordon Moore's kitchen to a canvas where every aspect of the environment is part of, in some manner or another, the embedded Internet of the future." — *Pat Gelsinger, CEO, VMware*

"After reading Dr. Kaur's book Transitioning Embedded Systems to Intelligent Environment, I followed my life for a day. I was truly amazed to find how intelligent embedded systems have taken over my life. The mobile phone/device, Internet connected TV, PS3, Satellite receiver, home appliances, automobile components, GPS systems, location mapping, Traffic control, RFIDs, EMRs, medical devices, etc. What if a hacker gained control of my pacemaker and decided to blackmail me? I am sure in due time these intelligent embedded systems will also have an attitude problem. Dr. Kaur has brought together an astonishing array of ideas in one place to stimulate thought, action, and future vision. She takes the readers on a very insightful journey."- *Deepak Mohan, Sr. Vice President, Symantec Corporation*

"Satwant Kaur is a visionary seeing far into the future. Yet, she describes the more than 100 applications made possible by Intel's embedded processors and platforms, for you to take your design to higher levels of intelligence today! This book belongs at the desk of every system developer and designer for decades to come." — *Desikan Bharathan, Principal Engineer, National Renewable Energy Laboratory*

"In her new book Transitioning Embedded Systems to Intelligent Environments, Dr. Satwant Kaur reveals that the technologies required to create an exciting world where intelligent environments enhance all aspects of daily life are not visions of the future, but exist today. With the application of human imagination and initiative, the possibilities are limitless." — *John Stafford, Director, Customer Connectivity, Quest Diagnostics Nichols Institute*

"Transitioning Embedded Systems to Intelligent Environments is a must-read for every student, scholar and soothsayer of the convergence phenomenon. I would highly recommend this book for system developers, enterprise management professionals, platform architects and, above all, for techno-entrepreneurs. The author has brought together an astonishing array of ideas in one place to stimulate thought, action and future vision." - *Subramaniam Ganesan, Professor of Engineering, Oakland University,*

"Many future gazers would be satisfied with proposing a single vision for the future but Dr. Kaur appears to be afflicted by visions, such is the breadth in scope of the technological possibilities that she highlights in this 'Journey Through Evolving Technologies.' What is perhaps more staggering is each possible future that Dr. Kaur discusses is grounded in solid technical thinking. Dr. Kaur considers not only the what, but also the how, leveraging Intel's war chest of technology innovation to hypothesize how her many visions of the future could become reality. I challenge the reader to find another analysis with the range of imagination to include 'robot swarms in the blood stream,' 'cargo management by smart railcars,' and the potential sensor and processor technology required to realize these possibilities." - *Parker Moss, Head of Strategy , GSMA*

"The Internet of Things will have yet unimaginable devices connect to the network. The scale of these networks will only be possible with technology innovations in software, systems and transitioning embedded systems to intelligent environments. This book discusses some of the applications in the Internet of Things and enabling technologies.- *Kelly Ahuja, SVP/GM, Chief Architect Service Provider Business, Cisco*

Table of Contents

Foreword by Pat Gelsinger, CEO, VMware

When Gordon Moore first saw the 4004 microprocessor that Intel had invented almost 40 years ago, he walked around his kitchen that night trying to imagine all the places for which it could add intelligence to every day devices in his home. He could envision them in his refrigerators and ovens and such throughout his home simply helping those appliances work better for the user.

If we fast-forward to today, not only do we have the power of the microprocessor but it is combined with the resources of the worldwide Internet and wireless technologies. Thus, it isn't only about adding intelligence to existing appliances of the home but connecting every aspect of our lives; our work, play, learn, travel and rest environments to an ever burgeoning set of networked resources.

Some have termed this the Internet of Things, others the Invisible Internet and finally I myself have chosen to refer to it as the Embedded Internet. Literally, where we move from one to two billion Internet connections largely numbered based on people connections to tens of billions of connections based on the integration of the Internet into every aspect of the world we live in.

It is against this backdrop that Dr. Satwant Kaur takes a fresh look at what is required to design and deliver embedded systems into the intelligent environments that are being built by the collective IT industry around us. She chooses to focus on the Intel products and the embedded x86 environment in part because that's her current place of employment. But more so, the Intel product line is increasingly finding itself as the platform of choice for embedded systems due to its wide availability and incredible breadth of software and tools. This is the case in large environments like storage systems and communications environments but increasingly and most interestingly into smaller and smaller devices as a result of the launch and thrust of the Intel® Atom™ processor and its embedded progeny.

In Transitioning Embedded Systems to *Intelligent Environments,* you will see Satwant's love for technology come pouring through the pages. As I have gotten to know her, she is a passionate individual who deeply desires a better world that is enabled through an ever-broadening use of technology. She lays out both a vision and data on the key technologies for the future of the embedded world. She has moved from Gordon Moore's kitchen to a canvas where every aspect of the environment is part of, in some manner or another, the embedded Internet of the future. Further her paints and paintbrushes are brought forth by Intel products and numerous examples of today's technology building blocks to help you the reader have a sense of how to navigate in designing and developing those embedded systems of tomorrow. Best of luck as you gather together these new learnings and apply them toward your design challenges and opportunities of tomorrow.

Pat Gelsinger
CEO, VMWare

Preface

My writing of this book *Transitioning Embedded Systems to Intelligent Environments* has been inspired by the major innovations that have been made possible by embedded technologies in last twenty-five years, ever since I created the first capacitor-manufacturing robot for small-scale industries.

My robot was a visionary emulation of human workers in small-scale industries who built capacitors with their hands one by one. However, the embedded system for the robot was built using Intel's 8088 processor, which was the size of a suitcase, had LED outputs and a numeric keypad, and required binary language programming. The robot could perform only one operation, which was to build capacitors to the microfarads specified.

This book is not a testimony of how the field of embedded systems has evolved over the last twenty-five years. Rather, like the robot, this book is a vision of intelligent environments. It details what the intelligent environment looks like, and how we get to that vision of intelligent environments.

There are many compelling reasons to change our surroundings to one with intelligent environments. Many technologies are propelling us well armed into that future. This book details the path to get to our vision. This book details 101 example intelligent environments and describes how various technologies enable each one to become a reality.

Satwant Kaur

About the Author

DR. SATWANT KAUR

FIRST LADY OF EMERGING TECHNOLOGIES®

Dr. Satwant Kaur is hailed as the "First Lady of Emerging Technologies®" in Silicon Valley, Media, and the industry worldwide. She is the author of "Transitioning Embedded Systems to Intelligent Environments"

Dr. Satwant Kaur has more than 20 years of proven success and innovation in the emerging technology arena. She currently serves as the Chief Technologist – Innovation for BSC account in the office of the CTO at Hewlett-Packard Company. Her professional positions have included: Strategist at the Office for the CTO at EMC; Platform Strategist in Intel Architecture Group at Intel; Director of Development at Symantec; Chief Architect (Allstate) at Computer Associates (CA Technologies); Chief Technology Architect at Quest Software (part of DELL); Chief Technology Officer for TIBCO and Management Consultant. Dr. Kaur has also served on the Board of Panacea Software and Expert Consultant for Thomson Reuters.

She was also Electrical Engineering Faculty Member at Idaho State University and Computer Science Faculty Member at Indian Institute of Technology, Delhi (IIT)

Hundreds of Radio Shows have broadcast her interviews. Her live Radio Show segment, "First Lady of Emerging Technologies®" on "Computers 2 Know" earned thousands of live audience. She has been interviewed by CBS, Huffington Post and her interviews have been broadcast on hundreds of CBS sites.

She is a sought after keynote speaker on emerging technologies at IEEE conferences on Consumer Electronics, IEEE embedded system workshops, Connected World Conference, and IIT global conference,

She is the author of IETE bi-monthly column "Pushing frontiers with the First Lady of Emerging Technologies®". imageSource magazine publishes monthly interviews with her. Dr. Kaur has been featured on front cover of "Mobile Development and Design", "Fierce Smart Grid", "Government Security News". She has been saluted as "Women of M2M" by the Connected World magazine on their annual list.

She received her doctorate in Mobile IP technologies from Oakland University in Oakland, Michigan. She also holds a Bachelor of Technology degree in Electrical Engineering with distinction from the Indian Institute of Technology in New Delhi, India.

Her email is: satwant@drsatwantkaur.com. Her website is: www.satwantkaur.com.

Her Book "Transitioning Embedded Systems to Intelligent Environments" can be purchased at amazon.com.

Acknowledgements

I dedicate this book to my incredible mentors, John Wei (Chief Technologist at Hewlett-Packard, Larry Schmidt (HP Fellow and Chief Technologist), Terry White (HP Fellow and Chief Technologist), Doug Davis (VP, Intel), Pat Gelsinger (CEO, VMware), Cathy Brune (CIO, Allstate), Subra Ganesan (Professor, Oakland University), Bill Merrow (VP, Computer Associates), and S N Maheshwari (Professor, IIT Delhi). Without their unconditional acceptance of me as their mentee, and the foundations they built in me, I would not have been the engineer that I am today. Let alone having written this book.

It has been my pleasure to write this book. I hope it will be yours to read it.
Thanks.
Dr. Satwant Kaur

1

A Vision of Intelligent Environments: 101 Scenarios

Introduction

An embedded system is a system that has intelligence built in for computing and decision-making. The most advanced embedded system is the human system. It uses eyes and ears as sensors, and limbs as controlled devices to interact with its environment. It can evaluate, compute, analyze, and arrive at correct decisions by using a brain as its processor.

Existing embedded systems emulate the human body. These special-purpose computing systems have tightly integrated hardware and software, connected to environment via actuators and sensors. Embedded systems incorporate a computer, usually a microprocessor or microcontroller, which simplifies system design and provides flexibility. The embedded system generally is not viewed as a computing element by itself, but instead performs a dedicated function. As such, embedded systems are often invisible as they are encapsulated within larger systems, and often the user of the device is not even aware that a computer is embedded.

Intelligent environments by contrast emulate an entire virtual army of humans, rather than an individual. The army can expand infinitely, and its ability to interact is infinite. The individual devices, like recruits, can be controlled, can talk to each other, are always on, and yet are invisible until and unless needed. The result is a pervasive and ubiquitous environment. It provides all kinds of information to us automatically or on demand. It seeks to assess, anticipate and address our needs. It interacts with us in a natural manner.

Intelligent environments' countless intelligent connected embedded devices help in every facet of life. There are so many dots that interact with you and with each other. When you draw the threads of interactions between these tiny dots and yourself and step back to look at a lower resolution, it becomes like a piece of fabric that envelopes you like a safety blanket. And at any point of time you can call upon the blanket to carry out desired tasks, to alert you to certain real-time events, to help you make the right decisions, to provide you with specific information, and to provide you with fused and analyzed information of real-time happenings around you.

Intelligent environments become the intelligence to connect us with all things around us, whether it is at home, in cars, in hospitals, or in our clothes. They are connected to the Internet with web services to interact in a mobile wireless world. Some examples of these interactions are information and decision making through the Internet, instant communication by voice or text, monitoring, and alerting. The key to intelligent environments is unparalleled intelligence in the embedded applications.

Let us go over the opportunities for all of us that lie ahead. Over 101 such scenarios are listed. Each of these describes how life within intelligent environments will look and feel like in the future. It also discusses the challenges that need to be addressed for us to get there, and some of the enabling Intel technologies.

Intelligent Energy Management Environments

Batteries with their limitation of lifetime and size are a thing of past. In intelligent environments, embedded devices upon which our lives depend are autonomous with their own embedded energy sources.

Embedded devices in intelligent environments harvest all needed power from larger unused power sources of the environment. Thus ambient energy is recycled and consumed on a continual basis. No energy is wasted.

Energy from Intelligent Environments

The sources of power from the environment can be photovoltaic energy from rays of sun, mechanical energy from vibration of machines, electromagnetic energy from antennas of radios or the energy from exercising of humans. It can also be thermal energy from temperature gradients or the kinetic energy. Other sources of power are wind, geothermal, and ocean waves. Transducers generate electricity by converting the vibrations on aircraft, the fluctuations of magnetic fields, the radio waves in the air, and environmental gradients in temperature. Sources of energy from intelligent environments include the following:

- Piezoelectric transducers convert mechanical stress into electrical energy
- Human motion: leg, arm, walking
- Acoustic noise
- Hydraulic pressure
- Walkways
- Vibration from engines
- Impact of falling raindrops
- Ocean waves

- Photovoltaic cells convert energy from sun to electrical energy
- Thunder actuators convert energy from thunder to electrical energy
- Electromagnetic energy: converts motion between magnetic flux to electrical energy
- Ambient radio frequency broadcasts from radio and television stations
- Electrostatic energy: converts motion between capacitor planes to electrical energy
- Vibrations change the value of variable capacitors
- Ambient radiation: radio transmitters in radio frequency identification (RFID) devices.
- Pressure gradient: wind turbine propelled by winds
- Kinetic energy: wrist watches powered by movement of the arm
- Metabolic energy: trees
- Bio energy
- Oxidation of blood sugars
- Blood pressure in humans
- Thermo electrics: converts heat to power with space temperature gradient
- Pyro electrics: converts heat to power with temporal temperature gradient

Scenario #1. Mechanical power from moving railway traffic is used to supply electrical power to embedded sensors that signal warning lights at crossings.

Scenario # 2. The energy transducers are integrated into our clothing so most of our motion is used for power harvesting.

Scenario #3. Embedded devices convert motion of ocean waves into electricity. This electricity is used by sensors inside the ocean for monitoring.

Scenario #4. Heat in automobile engine combustion is converted into electricity.

Scenario #5. Building structures have built-in absorbers and piezoelectric devices. The absorbers confine the vibration energy and the energy is automatically harvested by means of piezoelectric devices.

Scenario #6. User interfaces are human-powered. The power from the physical effort required to operate the user interface becomes the temporary power source for the embedded device. Light switches use the energy of the human toggle itself to wirelessly send the electric signal to the fixture in the ceiling.

Scenario #7. Energy created by humans on exercise machines is harnessed and channeled to power embedded entertainment systems in the exercise machines.

Scenario #8. The human body generates mechanical power by passive movements such as joint rotation, enforcement of body weight, vertical displacement of mass centers, and even elastic deformation of tissues. All these are harvested and used to power implanted medical devices and most electronic devices carried by humans.

Scenario #9. Power from ambient radio waves keeps all mobile devices powered. Ambient electromagnetic radiation that is emitted from Wi-Fi† transmitters, cell-phone antennas, and other sources creates enough electrical current to recharge mobile phones.

Scenario #10. Electromagnetic waves are converted into an electrical signal that generates power for wireless sensors, RFID tags, and consumer devices. These technologies for recharging sensors with dedicated radio signals work even from great distances.

Scenario #11. Radio frequency power harvesters are used to power passive RFID transponders. RF signals from antenna are used for harvesting.

Scenario #12. Solar cells are always embedded into the outer casings of all mobile devices. They also have batteries as backup for nighttime. That way energy is generated and stored whenever available.

Scenario #13. The solar-powered wireless gateways are remote communication nodes capable of running upon solar photovoltaic power, which power many remote wireless sensor networks and other remote computing and communications.

The power availability characteristics of power harvesters are very different from other power sources. They are perpetually available but in minimal strengths. This means that the characteristic of the devices that use them also has to change. That may entail a paradigm shift in the way energy is utilized. For example the cost of receiving a bit (perpetual listening mode) is far more than cost of transmitting a bit (demand-based transmission).

Some challenges in energy from intelligent environments are as follows:

- Collecting energy from a variety of gradients:
- Pressure gradient, temperature gradient, chemical gradient, and so on
- Solar harvesting efficiency: a fraction of the available energy is harvested
- Piezoelectric harvesting efficiency: energy captured per actuation of strain
- Devices must be sufficiently robust to withstand long-term exposure to hostile propagation environments
- Energy must be stored in such a way that devices can function in an uninterrupted manner even when collecting energy is not possible:
- Energy storage needs to be compact, efficient, low discharge rate, high energy density
- Providing energy and performance characteristics for higher level embedded devices
- Maximum energy storage capacity
- Currently available energy level
- Energy charge rate
- Energy consumption rate
- Range till which energy is available

Intelligent Energy Management (Facilities)

Table 1.1 describes an intelligent energy management wireless sensor network (WSN) and the corresponding enabling technologies from Intel.

Scenario #14. Wireless sensor networks are used to monitor, manage, and control patterns of energy consumption in homes, commercial buildings, industries, and utility power distribution grids. Intelligent connected platforms collect data from dozens of wireless sensors in a wireless sensor network. Analysis of the combined data is done through sensor fusion.

Scenario #15. Intelligent energy management systems provide building managers a highly granular view of energy consumption over time, enabling them to infer building workloads and activity levels. These systems also provide consumers insights into actual usage patterns that can enable them to respond to demand-based (peak/off-peak) billing models imposed by utilities.

Table 1.1   Intelligent Energy Management WSN

Intelligent Energy Management WSN	Enabling Intel Technologies
■ Instrumentation of full building is done, adding hundreds of low-cost battery-powered wireless sensors to monitor environmental parameters including temperature, humidity, and lighting. ■ Numerous tiny, extremely low-power sensors link together to form multi-hop, self-configuring dynamically routed wireless sensor networks. ■ Low power gateway server-router systems configure and manage the networks, collect, fuse, and analyze the data, and provide the right information to users and the right actuation to the network. ■ A Web services-based application performs sensor fusion analysis of data collected from networked sensors.	■ The embedded devices are a compact, low-power design based on an Intel® Atom™ processor Z5xx series and Intel® System Controller Hub (Intel SCH) US15W. This platform manages an IEEE 802.15.4 mesh network that can support large number of sensors. ■ Intel® architecture power management features enable a small-footprint fanless device ■ Gateway server-routers built on the embedded Intel architecture platforms provide the processing intelligence and connectivity to collect, manage, and analyze large volumes of data. These are tiny wireless computing platform with a processor, memory, flash memory storage, I/O, and radio components.

Smart Grid Substations and Smart Meters

Table 1.2 describes smart grid substations and the corresponding enabling technologies from Intel.

Scenario #16. Smart meters are used in homes that help users make decisions in real time about how to control costs.

Scenario #17. Smart grid substations respond to variations in electricity supply and demand in real-time to ensure that global utilities can provide energy with quality and availability.

Scenario #18. Smart grid substations provide energy efficiencies as the electrical grid communicates and configure the most efficient energy flow routes through power substations.

Scenario #19. Smart grid substations collect data related to energy demand and supply in real time.

Scenario #20. Smart grid substations communicate with the home's power management system to turn off noncritical systems during an energy shortage.

Scenario #21. The smart grid is an IP-based network. Substation units deployed at the substation communicate over an IP network with IP-enabled smart meters at homes and businesses. These IP communications provide real-time data that allows electric power utilities to accurately measure demand, as well as quantify electricity pushed back into the grid from roof-top photovoltaic and other domestic renewable micro-generation systems.

Scenario #22. The energy companies charge more for peak time's usage. Thus the consumers voluntarily shift electric power usage to off-peak periods. This also helps utilities get the most from their existing generation infrastructure, while saving hundreds of megawatts of power and avoiding the capital cost of new generation plants.

Scenario #23. Smart grid substations utilize predictive technology and self-healing networks that meet consumers' energy demands and also provide access to green alternative energy sources.

Table 1.2   Smart Grid Substations

Smart Grid Substations	Enabling Intel Technologies
■ Smart grids work with smart grid substations to help collect energy usage and generation related data in real time. ■ Substation units deployed at the substation communicate over IP networks with interoperable smart meters at homes and businesses. ■ This two-way IP-based communication with smart meters enables substation control equipment to regulate voltage levels to match demand requirements and perform power factor analysis that can help optimize the quality of electric power and bring efficiencies in the electrical grid system. ■ As an IP-based network, the smart grid makes use of reusable communications infrastructure building blocks, standards-based protocols, and best known methods to accelerate development of new applications and solutions.	■ The smart grid is an IP based network based on Intel® architecture. Industrial PCs based on scalable embedded Intel processors can collect data in real time. ■ Fault detection devices, power quality monitoring, electric power meters, automated switch gear, substation network routers and gateways, and other substation equipment can be based on based on Intel® Atom™ and Intel® Core™2 Duo processor. ■ Intel® Active Management Technology (Intel AMT) can provide IT support personnel with out-of-band system access irrespective of the device state. ■ Intel AMT can remotely discover, heal, and protect computing assets, including remote system isolation and recovery in the event of an operating system failure. ■ Intel AMT MP System Defense Manager can proactively block incoming threats, contain infected clients before they impact the network and alert IT when critical software agents are removed. ■ Intel® Trusted Execution Technology (Intel® TXT) can improve security by defending against attacks and protecting the integrity of data moving through an embedded system. ■ Intel® Virtualization Technology (Intel® VT can provide optimal system utilization through system consolidation by means of multiple virtual machines. ■ Intel architecture platforms enable the substations to communicate with widely distributed electric generation facilities, such as wind farms and roof-mounted photovoltaic panels, to help balance electricity load on the grid.

Smart Wind Turbines

Table 1.3 describes smart wind turbines and the corresponding enabling technologies from Intel.

Scenario #24. Intelligent, connected wind turbines provide new sources of electricity. Massive intelligent wind turbines are one of the large sources of electricity per year that replaces electric power equivalent to burning large amounts of coal. Thus there is energy savings and cleaner air.

Table 1.3   Smart Wind Turbines

Smart Wind Turbines	Enabling Intel Technologies
■ Smart wind turbines need intelligent embedded wind turbine controllers. ■ Localized intelligence, in the form of embedded wind turbine controllers, control turbine vane pitch, rotation, and other variables in response to real-time information including changing wind conditions and electrical load requirements, without human intervention. ■ Network sensors mounted on the wind turbine communicate data to the embedded computer to monitor operating parameters including bearing temperature and vibration. ■ Diagnostic data for each turbine is monitored in real time by technicians in a regional control center.	■ The energy efficiency of the embedded Intel® architecture components can enable wind turbine controllers, which require sealed fanless construction to withstand demanding environmental conditions, and anti-vibration capabilities. ■ Based on the 7-watt ultra low voltage Intel® Celeron® processor or the 10-watt Intel® Pentium® M processor LV 738, each turbine-mounted controller can support four 10/100Base-T Fast Ethernet ports, in addition to a wide range of DC power sources.

Smart Home Displays

Table 1.4 describes smart home displays and the corresponding enabling technologies from Intel.

Scenario #25. Smart home displays are in-home real-time energy monitoring and control systems that help users control costs. Power utilities have a demand response monitoring system that encourages reductions in peak energy demand by displaying real-time energy usage and utility pricing. Providing real-time information linked to such dynamic pricing helps consumers who want to cut energy costs.

Scenario #26. Smart home displays help customers manage energy consumption by displaying real-time data on their current energy consumption, real-time costs, and the potential savings that can be achieved by turning off or rescheduling the use of appliances.

Table 1.4   Smart Home Displays

Smart Home Displays	Enabling Intel Technologies
■ Smart home displays can display real-time energy usage and pricing as graphical displays, centrally control all thermostats, and communicate demand response event notification.	■ Smart home displays can be powered by embedded Intel processors including the Intel® Core™2 Duo processor and Intel® Atom™ processor.
■ They also tell consumers how their personal energy consumption compares to similar households, including tabulations of average usage in the neighborhood and the lowest usage by any household.	■ Low power is key to the application, since smart home displays will run 24x7 in the home. The Intel Atom processor combines energy-saving advanced sleep states
■ They also connect with photovoltaic solar systems, and provide a graphic real-time indicator of energy savings achieved in homes and commercial sites, such as stores and supermarkets.	■ Energy monitoring functionality can also be integrated with consumer electronics to allow graphically rich information to be displayed on a TV or IP media phone, based on the Intel Atom processor.

Smart Lights

Table 1.5 describes smart lights and the corresponding enabling technologies from Intel.

Scenario #27. Smart lights save energy by monitoring traffic, weather conditions, time of the day, amount of darkness, so that only the amount of lighting that is necessary is provided.

Scenario #28. Intelligent adaptive street lighting gives utilities flexible control over lighting levels at each pole to match actual local requirements, such as automobile and pedestrian traffic volume, ambient light levels and weather conditions.

Scenario #29. Smart lights enable utilities to monitor individual street lights to anticipate lamp and photocell failures before they occur.

Scenario #30. Intelligent street lights connected over networks provide various capabilities, such as measuring and analyzing power consumption, turning on flashing street lights in emergency situations, and controlling programmable electronic signage mounted on light poles.

Table 1.5   Smart Street Lights

Smart Street Lights	Enabling Intel Technologies
■ Wirelessly connected sensors, one on each light pole, connect through a self-configuring mesh network to access the gateway device. ■ The gateway device can support hundreds of sensors and then securely transmit real-time data to a protected server. ■ Each street light can be programmed to adjust light output to traffic or weather conditions to save electricity. ■ Wireless gateways support cellular network connectivity, allowing direct control of street lights by authorized personnel using a cell phone. ■ Software applications are used for monitoring, data analytics, and control, without replacing field-mounted access equipment.	■ The gateway devices can be powered by energy-efficient Intel® Atom™ processors. ■ The Intel Atom processor in industrial temperature version can be used to extend the benefits of Intel® microarchitecture to access gateways consisting of small form factor, thermally constrained, and fanless sealed box computers designed to withstand extremes of temperature, dust, and humidity. ■ The use of Intel® architecture hardware, from central servers to hundreds of pole-mounted gateway devices throughout a city, enables public works authorities and power utilities to base their street lighting infrastructure on a consistent software code base, including leading real-time operating systems and tool chains.

Intelligent Home Environments

Intelligent home environments have autonomous service robots, intelligent machines that can sense, perceive, recognize, think, and act to perform tasks in the world all by themselves, with no human controlling them.

Underlying robot technologies that enable such machines are locomotion (wheeled, legged, flying, swimming, and crawling robots), learning, manipulation (both arms and hands), grasping, localization, navigation, and mapping.

Robots are adapted and customized to do any number of human-like tasks that are boring, time consuming, difficult, or dangerous for human beings or have to be performed in harsh conditions. For example, they can entertain by playing games with the children, do boring activities like guide visitors to the restroom, and security related activities like frightening off intruders. They can do highly skilled activities like teaching how to play musical instruments like the piano. They do difficult jobs like carrying factory goods, mundane tasks like promoting new products, and dangerous jobs like monitoring hospital radiation.

Scenario #31. Human-like awareness and behaviors allow robots to adapt to their surroundings. These live looking robots have personalities that can be programmed.

Scenario #32. Automation of household stock management eliminates running out of stock on anything. For example, the refrigerator can talk to grocery store systems and order replenishments so it is always well stocked.

Robots in the Household

Table 1.6 describes autonomous household robots and the corresponding enabling technologies from Intel.

Scenario #33. Fully autonomous robots do a variety of very human-like tasks, such as playing games and guiding visitors. They adapt to changing conditions in their environment. Such fully autonomous robots can work in environments built for people instead of in walled cells or specially-marked corridors.

Table 1.6   Autonomous Houschold Robots

Autonomous Household Robots	Enabling Intel Technologies
◼ Autonomous household robots can learn their operating environment through the use of mapmaking software, employing laser scans and measurements to create a model of their surroundings. ◼ Robot programmers can use drag-and-drop software to assign the robot certain tasks and behaviors specific to that environment. ◼ Robots can be programmed using pre-defined behaviors available in the robot builder platform library. And by using a graphical programming environment, more complex functions and behaviors can be added and integrates with accessories and off-board devices.	◼ Intel's multi-core embedded processors can provide the powerful multi-threaded, multi-processor performance needed to manage the sensors, analytical tools, and high-level software that the robot needs to understand and react to its environment. ◼ Intel's virtualization can enable the flexibility that robots need to run on both real-time feedback and enterprise applications.

Home Security with Smart Video Analytics

Unobtrusive identification and security is a way of life. You can walk into your house without opening locks. The system recognizes you through your voice, face, or quick thumbprint. The environment knows exactly where you were on all days, and can help track your family.

Scenario #34. Visualization and speech recognition instead of keyboards: there is no need to type. Other more natural and secure ways to interact are part of every embedded device.

Scenario #35. Security systems are based on face recognition. Burglaries and auto thefts are prevented. Homes open up and cars start up only if facial recognition is successful.

Scenario #36. Based on viewer's position and viewing angle, the television orients itself for the best viewing experience for the person watching it.

Scenario #37. Profile-based management of household appliances enables individual bath water temperature settings for each family member to be automatically set.

Scenario #38. Laptops, based on biometric identification, only work for the owner. Sensors on the keyboard and screen make sure that only the owner can view/write using it.

Intelligent Industrial Environments

Intelligent industrial environments are secure. They have self-learning autonomous robots. These autonomous robots work as farmers, sentries, and so on.

Security with Smart Threat Management

Table 1.7 describes network security appliances and the corresponding enabling technologies from Intel.

Scenario #39. Intelligent environments need increased network bandwidth to serve intelligent connected devices. This places heavy new security demands on the communications infrastructure. Smart and unified threat management takes care of making embedded Internet fast and secure. In addition to network edge devices, enterprise users place network security appliances between internal subnets to help manage and control content. These unified threat management systems provides cost-effective and environmentally friendly solutions.

Table 1.7   Network Security Appliances

Network Security Appliances	Enabling Intel Technologies
■ Enterprise network security is evolving from protecting the network perimeter to providing comprehensive, content-based security to counter threats at all network layers, including those that may not be checked by traditional stateful firewalls. As it handles increasing volumes of sensitive data, the embedded Internet will impose similar requirements. ■ Comprehensive, content-based security approaches require deep packet inspection capable of detecting threats that masquerade as legitimate application-layer traffic. ■ Just as server consolidation is driving down equipment cost and footprint in data centers, security applications are being consolidated onto high-end network security platforms. Such consolidation can eliminate the cost of maintaining multiple point-security products and drive down total cost of ownership.	■ Network security appliances based in Intel® architecture can cover all of the major network security categories from firewall through web application protection, including the ability to run hundreds of virtual firewalls in a single system. ■ Enterprise networks, with speeds exceeding 40 gigabits per second (Gbps), can be protected by Intel® Xeon® processor-based platforms. ■ Small form factor security appliances use the Intel® EP80579 Integrated Processor with Intel® QuickAssist Technology, a system-on-chip (SOC) that provides an automated, all-in-one security solution. ■ Intel architecture enables security appliances capable of providing scalable performance within a low power envelope while handling a growing variety of security tasks in a single server blade or chassis. ■ Security solutions that can be quickly updated with new security policies, monitoring strategies, and security applications.

Autonomous Manufacturing Robots

Examples of Autonomous Robots are underwater monitoring robots, mine hunting robots, walking machines with legs, and humanoid robots. Table 1.8 describes autonomous manufacturing robots and the corresponding enabling technologies from Intel.

Scenario #40. Autonomous industrial robots are found on the factory floor. New generations of intelligent multi-axis robotic arms incorporate 3D machine vision and video analytics software to improve manufacturing process efficiency, while making the factory floor a safer place for human workers.

Table 1.8   Autonomous Manufacturing Robots

Autonomous Manufacturing Robots	Enabling Intel Technologies
■ Autonomous manufacturing robots need to combine multi-axis motion control circuitry, video-based machine vision, input from networks of embedded sensors, and the latest sophisticated software. ■ They need to analyze real-time data from onboard machine vision systems, control up to 12 axes of rotation with extreme precision, and process data streams generated by networks of connected sensors. Video analytics software enables robots to recognize changes in their environment and instantly respond in the appropriate way. The ultra low power consumption of platforms enables smart robots and other devices to function reliably in the factory environment, with enhanced mobility.	■ Embedded industrial platforms based on Intel® Xeon® and Intel® Core™ 2 Duo processors provide the processing performance that industrial robots need. ■ Embedded Intel platforms are enabling designers to replace multiple processors with a single processor that is capable of analyzing multiple sensor inputs for applications including industrial assembly tasks, quality control measurements, and safety. ■ Advanced embedded Intel® architecture platform technologies can provide the robust computing capabilities that enable industrial control and automation equipment to quickly and easily share data with IT infrastructure in today's digital industries. ■ Robots and other real-time devices built on Intel® AMT-enabled platforms can be remotely accessed, maintained, and updated with new software to combine production volume and flexibility. Virtualization allows both a graphical user interface and a real-time operating system for deterministic processes to run on the same machine without risk of one system impacting the other.

Intelligent Farming by Robots

Table 1.9 describes autonomous agriculture robots and the corresponding enabling technologies from Intel.

Scenario #41. Human beings no longer toil on farms. Farming is done through remote control with robotic farming equipment. Several robots drive several tractors at once, plow the lands, till fields, plant seeds, dispense fertilizers, and harvest crops.

Scenario #42. Equipped with GPS navigation equipment and onboard sensors to analyze soil conditions, a robot can measure soil characteristics on the fly at the front end, and then use the results of the soil analysis to dispense the precise application of fertilizer—all in a single pass as it traverses the field. This technique maximizes the productivity of farm equipment while minimizing the use of farm chemicals, conserving fuel, and potentially increasing crop production by providing ideal applications of fertilizers and water.

Scenario #43. Robot farmers have machine vision systems for collision avoidance and crop monitoring. Other sensors can monitor the fuel state and operating condition of the tractor and its attached implements and send read-outs to the farm's central monitoring station. Automatic alerts generated by Robots can enable farm operators to perform preventive maintenance to avoid costly equipment breakdowns.

Scenario #44. Human machine interface (HMI) systems, whether in the tractor's cab or displayed on a monitor back at the farm office, can be identical for every vehicle on the farm. This makes it easy for a single operator to supervise, and if necessary control several autonomous vehicles simultaneously from an office or a mobile computer in a pickup truck.

Scenario #45. Automation of tedious tasks such as landscaping, mowing, and fertilizing, decorative horticulture, dead leaf removal and weeding are automated.

Table 1.9   Autonomous Agriculture Robots

Autonomous Agriculture Robots	Enabling Intel Technologies
■ Perform complex, fast analysis and calculate optimum chemical application rates in real time. ■ Contain database of statistical information of different micro-sites within a field, which are correlated with crop monitoring data and satellite imagery as it grows. ■ Power the vehicle's sophisticated human-machine interface (HMI), which shows a real-time map of the field, and provides data on soil conditions, water, crop characteristics, and other variables. ■ Do GPS positioning, navigation, steering, onboard connectivity, and WLAN-based communication to the farm's monitoring center.	■ The energy efficient performance and low thermal characteristics of Intel® Atom™ processors can be used for fanless, convection cooled, small-footprint onboard embedded automation and control computers designed to withstand temperature, dust, heat, humidity and vibration. ■ Intel Atom processors Z530 and Z510 and industrial temperature versions Z510P, Z530P, Z510PT, Z520PT can be used for developing solutions for harsh, mobile environments like farm and other commercial vehicles.

Some of the challenges of autonomous robots include the following:

- Design of data capture devices appropriate to the required functions: camera, sonar, odometer, tilt sensor
- Weather adaptability: heat, rain, snow, humidity, extreme temperatures
- Real-time vision and vision analytics
- Computational architectures for autonomous systems

- Distributed architectures for learning, control, and adaptation
- Integration with mobile sensor networks for optimal environmental sensing
- Sensor fusion
- Self-calibration and self-repair
- Self reproducing (replicating) intelligent machines
- Autonomous robot mapping and navigation
- Topological representation of environment
- Terrain mapping and recognition
- Estimate of path, position
- Error bounds on localization
- Ambiguities in mapping
- Uncertainties in navigation
- Course correction: nature of course correction in three dimensions; speed at which course can be changed
- Acoustics and optical sensing of complex environments
- Not just sensing but perception to be self sufficient
- Autonomous behavior integrated with real time control of robots
- Robot building and training platforms
- They can be trained (or retrained) for specific functions

Intelligent Health Environments

Technologies have brought all medical facilities close to patients, at all times and at all places. Whether it be doctors, nurses, lab technicians, facilities, medical small devices, or medical large equipment. And this care, diagnosis, and treatment are done in real time, thanks to technologies.

Lightweight Intel embedded systems and wireless technologies have enabled remote healthcare. Thus medical exams in doctors office can now extend into patient monitored at all times for certain health conditions.

The miniaturization of medical devices with embedded Intel hardware has enabled them to be connected to the patients at all times in an invisible manner.

The continuous sensing is done by small wireless sensors that can be built upon Intel Atom processors.

Numerous Bluetooth† wireless biometric sensors connected to patient can provide critical patient medical information to decision makers at remote.

Intel's advanced technologies have enabled the patient data to be to be available to medical teams in real time and in a secure manner.

Intel's high performance processors allow visual analysis of the large amounts of data generated by a multitude of sensors to be presented to medical teams in a cohesive manner, enabling them to make accurate and timely diagnosis and treatment.

Effectively we have doctors everywhere. Instead of patients going to doctors, telehealth has enabled doctors to come to patients. More diseases are now managed more effectively for patients in their natural surroundings.

Not only are medical teams available to consult with remote patients on a continual basis, but even computing infrastructure interacts with automated remote medical devices of patients. This communication presents an added piece of patient data for medical consultants to base their judgments on.

Even medical labs are available for remote patients; samples can be taken remotely and, using technology advancements, results can be processed in faraway labs.

Advanced technologies ensure that these interactions from remote locations are kept isolated from each other for different patients. Technology advancements enable security and privacy in such sensitive information handling.

Scenario #46. Emergency medical teams use intelligent wireless medical systems as tools that they carry on person or in ambulances.

Scenario #47. The doctors can be miles away, but they can still provide services remotely even when the patient is at home or mobile being brought to hospital.

Scenario #48. Wireless diagnostic tools bring medical services to people in remote villages.

Scenario #49. Medical machines are miniaturized with connectivity/access to medical labs. For example, electrocardiogram (ECG), stress test machines, brainwave monitor or electroencephalogram (EEG), blood test meter, insulin pumps are hooked invisibly on body by the patient.

Scenario #50. Mobile medical diagnostic tools are used in hospitals, to continuously monitor patients. These diagnostic tools can be attached to everyone when they are admitted.

Scenario #51. Personal health monitoring sensors saves lives. Human embedded medical devices scan and monitor biological systems to provide proactive treatments. Body functions like heartbeat; chemical levels in blood; and the state of viral infection are constantly monitored for good health. Miniaturized EEG ensures that any potential seizure cases are detected and proactively reported.

Scenario #52. Wearable remote devices are used for monitoring and treating patients. Recording of data is continuous and is gathered remotely; it reduces human errors that can happen during outpatient care.

Scenario #53. Automated abnormal medical incident reporting triggers proactive treatment remotely and save lives.

Scenario #54. Lab equipment like microscopes have embedded systems that analyze the sample. The microscope takes an image of the sample, compares against databases of known diseases, and transfers results to doctors for further review.

Scenario #55. Bandage-like pedometers continuously monitor and reports vital body stats like heartbeats, calories burnt during the day, and body temperature.

Scenario #56. Hearing aids translate spoken foreign languages in real time. Accent neutralization is done by hearing aids that neutralize the spoken language accent and help understand all dialects. Hearing aids warn the visually impaired of any upcoming hazards that have been proactively detected.

Scenario #57. Robotic muscles allow paraplegics to function normally. Robotic prosthetics can be powered by the body's own energy. Robotic muscles allow paraplegics to function normally. These prosthetics need power to operate. For example prosthetic feet provide a boost push-off as the ankle touches ground.

Scenario #58. Service robots provide medical assistance to elderly and disabled in their homes.

Mobile Diagnostics for Emergency Responders

Table 1.10 describes remote emergency doctors and the corresponding enabling technologies from Intel.

Scenario #59. Intelligent wireless medical diagnostic systems help critical patients requiring emergency surgeries by minimizing the time it takes to bring them to the appropriate medical facilities.

Table 1.10   Remote Emergency Doctors

Remote Emergency Doctors	Enabling Intel Technologies
■ Intelligent wireless medical systems provide first-responders with new tools to speed the diagnosis of heart conditions that require emergency cardiac catheterization. ■ Minimizing the transit time from the field to the nearest catheterization laboratory can save lives of cardiac patients. ■ Since only some hospital trauma units are equipped with cardiac catheterization laboratory containing the requisite imaging equipment, the ability of EMTs to select the closest destination is a critical issue. ■ GPS-equipped systems help route emergency vehicles to the nearest facility and help EMTs alert the hospital, so patients may be taken directly into the cardiac catheterization center, bypassing the emergency room.	■ Portable computers based on Intel® Core2™ Duo processors and touch-screen embedded computing devices based on the Intel® Atom™ processor are used to collect, analyze, and transmit data which can confirm the need for cardiac catheterization. ■ Intel® architecture mobile devices provide performance, communications, and security needed to perform critical emergency medical procedures. ■ Devices powered by the Intel Core 2 Duo processor support commercial, off-the-shelf software solutions and remote manageability to keep systems working reliably. ■ Intel® Trusted Execution Technology provides hardware extensions that help protect against software-based attacks and protect the integrity of data moving through an embedded medical system.

Remote Patient Care

Table 1.11 describes how doctors save lives remotely and the corresponding enabling technologies from Intel.

Scenario #60. Doctors save lives remotely with their telepresence near the patient. The patient not only has a doctor but every diagnostic tool and every analysis lab at the bedside, no matter where the patient is. All the vital signs are remotely monitored in real time. All the medical samples are analyzed in real time. All the treatment is administered in real time. All this happens sometimes even without a hospital, a lab, or a doctor in the vicinity.

Scenario #61. All fire departments and ambulance crews use embedded technologies in compact mobile diagnostic equipment to transmit patient vital signs and diagnostic data in real time to doctors waiting for the patient at hospitals.

Scenario #62. Two-way communication of biometric data is used for expanded mobile treatment, either on the scene or en route in the ambulance, based upon the advice of an emergency room physician.

Scenario #63. With mobile digital mammography, women in rural communities also get the screening. Mobile vans equipped with digital mammography lets rural women quickly have their mammograms performed and read by remote radiologists. Remote radiologists can detect a possibly cancerous or suspicious spot immediately after the patient has her digitized mammogram.

Scenario #64. Clinicians use videoconferencing to remotely communicate with each other and patients.

Scenario #65. Digitized health records provide remote specialists with complete information about their patients

Scenario #66. Digital medical images from picture-archiving systems and even digital cameras are making a wide range of information available to doctors about patients from afar.

Scenario #67. Mobile healthcare sends text messaging services to remind people to take medications.

Scenario #68. Pills with edible computer chips send signals to a skin patch, which transmits data to a doctor's cell phone or computer. The information helps doctors track when patients take their medicines and whether there are adverse reactions.

Table 1.11   Doctors Save Lives Remotely

Doctors Save Lives From Remote	Enabling Intel Technologies
■ The availability of real-time biometric data over wireless networks lets doctors advise ambulance crews while the emergency teams are still on the scene, or en route with patients to the nearest hospital that is best equipped to handle the case.	■ Portable computers with Intel® Core™2 Duo processor-based platforms provide emergency personnel with mobile diagnostic capabilities. Mobile applications can be easily and securely connected with the hospital's Intel® architecture–based IT infrastructure.
■ This technology allows real-time analysis in the first critical moments of an emergency case. Remote diagnostic technology enables an even deeper analysis based on the patient's existing medical records.	■ Intel® Active Management Technology enables remote manageability to keep fleets of mobile diagnostic computers updated with the latest software.
■ Enhancements in energy-efficient processing performance place computing intelligence into the hands of emergency medical response technicians, allowing them to collect, analyze, and transmit data in new ways.	■ Intel® Virtualization Technology enables one ambulance-based system to function as multiple virtual systems, to run real-time data analysis software on the scene, and also provide doctors with the data they need.
	■ Intel® Trusted Execution Technology protects the integrity of data moving through the system.

Remote Medical Laboratory Analysis

Table 1.12 describes virtual lab doctors and the corresponding enabling technologies from Intel.

Scenario #69. Infectious diseases are a thing of past. With portable lab kits connected with remote labs, any disease is immediately identified and reported, and so infectious diseases have no chance to spread.

Scenario #70. Wirelessly connected diagnostic tools, such as portable microscope kits equipped with USB cameras and connected devices to analyze blood samples, bring advanced medical services to people even when where there are no medical labs or physicians in proximity. Intelligent diagnostic tools enable medical technicians to transmit patient data to physicians at a regional medical center for analysis. Anyone can submit a blood sample, and high resolution photomicrographs of slides can be instantly transmitted over a cellular network or satellite uplink to the pathology lab in a regional medical center. With an accurate diagnosis, on-scene medical personnel can provide recommended treatment and public health services.

Table 1.12   Virtual Lab Doctors

Virtual Lab Doctors	Enabling Intel Technologies
■ Wirelessly connected diagnostic tools include portable microscope kits. ■ The diagnostic device is linked to a microscope on one side. The microscope is fitted with a USB camera that takes digital photomicrographs of a blood or tissue sample and passes it to an embedded device for an analysis. ■ Embedded analytics is used to identify special marker cells for malaria and other blood-borne diseases. After generating the report, the device sends the results, encrypted in an email, to a pathologist at a regional medical center.	■ Embedded Intel® architecture enables a range of portable medical imaging devices and other equipment such as portable wirelessly connected ECG monitors, ultrasound, and blood analysis units, to quickly process data on-site and transmit the results to doctors and pathologists for analysis. ■ Intel® Active Management Technology (Intel® AMT) allows IT professionals to proactively monitor remote medical equipment systems for issues and install software patches and upgrades to keep the equipment operating under field conditions. Intel® Trusted Execution Technology (Intel® TXT) is a set of hardware extensions that improves security and protects data integrity through protected execution and memory spaces.

Intelligent Biomedical Monitoring and Control

Table 1.13 describes intelligent biomedical wireless sensor networks (WSNs) and the corresponding enabling technologies from Intel.

Scenario #71. Patients are monitored for the body's vital signs and other body functions, regardless of whether they are in a hospital, at home, in long-term care, or in other locations. The wireless sensor devices used to monitor are programmed to process the vital sign data and raise an alert condition when a particular vital sign (such as heart rate, oxygen saturation, or ECG data) falls outside of normal parameters.

Scenario #72. Patient's safety-critical functions, such as controlling infusion pumps or monitoring a patient's vital signs during surgery, are all done through automatic use of sensors and actuators thus minimizing human error.

Scenario #73. Customized patient-specific wireless vital signs and other health monitoring enable patients to walk corridors and visiting areas without being constrained by wires.

Table 1.13 Intelligent Biomedical WSNs

Intelligent Biomedical WSNs	Enabling Intel Technologies
■ An embedded computing platform with embedded and virtualization technologies used as a unifying base station for the network of body sensors. ■ Multiple applications consolidated on a single platform to reduce complexity, improve reliability, save cost, and shrink the physical footprint. ■ Multiple operating systems and applications execute simultaneously with a high level of code and data separation. I/O virtualization enables securely assigning specific I/O devices to specific operating systems. This capability offers more data protection for medical systems, integrating sensors from various vendors, because one application cannot receive another application's sensor data.	■ Hardware-assisted Intel® Virtualization Technology (Intel®VT) is combined with hypervisor software, to connect over several Bluetooth wireless sensors. ■ The hypervisor isolates each virtual instance by providing hardware protection to every partition with its own virtual addressing space. In addition, it guarantees resource availability, such as memory and CPU cycles, to each partition, so that no software can fully consume the scheduled memory or time resources of the other partitions.

Smart Hidden Medical Devices on the Body

Medical treatments are proactive. Most monitoring devices are so small that patients can carry them invisibly. Intelligent devices on the body include EEG (brain) and ECG (heart) monitor and knee braces. Table 1.14 describes virtual monitoring devices and the corresponding enabling technologies from Intel.

Scenario #74. Heart and brain patients carry wear a small lightweight wirelessly connected ECG or electroencephalogram (EEG) monitor that cannot even be seen by others. These monitors can proactively analyze data and wirelessly alert a doctor to the warning signs of a seizure or a heart attack before it occurs.

Scenario #75. Electroencephalogram (EEG) patterns that record the electrical activity of the brain are associated with certain neurological events, such as seizures. Analyzing brainwave patterns prior to an event may allow medical caregivers to anticipate or possibly even prevent it from happening.

Scenario #76. Smart knee braces are embedded with motion sensors with which physicians monitor rehabilitating patients remotely after they've been discharged from the hospital. As patients exercise, the knee braces wirelessly send the data to the doctor for view on a desktop, mobile, or handheld device.

Table 1.14   Virtual Monitoring Devices

Virtual Monitoring Devices	Enabling Intel Technologies
■ The review of large data sets like those produced by a multi-channel EEG recorder employs complex diagnostic algorithms and can be extremely time-consuming. Multiple EEG sensors and up to 64 data channels generate huge volumes of raw data. Extracting meaningful information requires a great deal of processing power. ■ Placing processing intelligence closer to the patient eliminates the need to transmit large volumes of raw data for later analysis. If a boundary condition is exceeded, an alert can be quickly transmitted to the patient's doctor.	■ Ultra-low-power, small-footprint embedded Intel® architecture devices and small footprint platforms based on the Intel® Atom™ processor enable gains in energy-efficient performance.

Intelligent Transportation Environments

Intelligence is embedded into the physical transportation infrastructure consisting of cars, highways, and terminals. This has increased capacity, efficiency, safety, and security for travelers.

Transportation is intelligent. Roads are smart. Highways are smart. Cars are smart. Road signs are smart. Rails are smart. Intelligent transportation prevents accidents. Highways have sensors that actively participate in traffic management. Weather sensor networks further bring intelligence to the roadway traffic management.

Ad hoc networks are used for communications between vehicles and between vehicles and roadside equipment in vicinity. Passengers in vehicles can receive and relay others messages through the wireless network. Collision warning, road sign alarms, and in-place traffic view is all available to the driver.

Passengers have multimedia and Internet connectivity facilities, all provided through wireless connectivity of each car.

Scenario #77. Collisions are detected based on video analytics and automated collision reporting.

Scenario #78. Optimal capacity usage is ensured in real time by smart automobiles, intelligent highways, and systems adaptive to real-time demand. The demand is comprehended from the forecasts based on environmental monitoring sensors. Thus, intelligence in cars, highways, and other smart devices together make dynamic load routing decisions possible based on real-time demand and real-time available capacity.

Scenario #79. If the highways sense a hazard in the immediate vicinity, they signal your car to ensure your safety by activating a warning system and/or engaging emergency brakes.

Scenario #80. Airport security is largely unmanned since recognition and scanning is automatic. Signs personalized to you guide you to your flight.

Vehicle Inspections by Smart Roads

Table 1.15 describes vehicle inspections by smart roads and the corresponding enabling technologies from Intel.

Scenario #81. Smart Roads inspect your tires as you drive. If tires are worn out, are losing tread or have a puncture, you are alerted while driving with your car beeping.

Scenario #82. Cameras are installed on roads to automatically monitor tire conditions. Based on the tire condition, the smart roads determine safe speed limits to drive on the road during current weather conditions, whether rain or shine.

Scenario #83. Smart roads perform regular measurement of tire tread depth of vehicles. They can even distinguish snow tires from regular tires. Authorities use this information to alert drivers that their tires need replacement via a roadside display.

Scenario #84. Traffic safety is paramount, on the highway, road sensors communicate with your car to ensure your car has fulfilled all regulations of maintenance. You receive notices in the mail if the tire state mandated by regulations is not maintained.

Scenario #85. Road security is based on environment conditions, so environments are also monitored.

Table 1.15   Vehicle Inspection by Smart Roads

Vehicle Inspection by Smart Roads	Enabling Intel Technologies
■ A sophisticated roadway device uses advanced laser triangulation to measure tread wear. ■ A digital high-speed smart 3D camera embedded in the road looks up and captures the laser line-illuminated tire surface and records 3D profiles of it. ■ The smart 3D camera provides information via Ethernet cable or wireless LAN to activate warning systems, license plate readers, cameras, or barriers.	■ The parallel processing power of an Intel® Core2™ Duo processor in the smart 3D camera required image processing speed to calculate the tread depth of a tire in just a little more than two milliseconds. ■ A smart 3D camera and its Intel processor require no fans and have no moveable components, thus it is maintenance free and ideal for road environments where shock and constant vibrations are expected.

Traffic Control by Smart Highways

Table 1.16 describes traffic control by smart highways and the corresponding enabling technologies from Intel.

Scenario #86. Smart highways have sensors along their edges and immediately know about any traffic accident on the highway.

Scenario #87. Smart highways call emergency response teams as needed to the highway and manage traffic in emergencies.

Scenario #88. Smart highways communicate with smart cars and inform them about any problems on their route ahead.

Scenario #89. Smart cars calculate an alternate route and helps travelers arrive at destination safely and on time.

Scenario #90. Smart highways use video-based collision detection as well as video-based collision reporting.

Scenario #91. Smart highways detect bad weather condition using sensors.

Scenario #92. Smart highways enforce speed control (through smart cars) on highways to help avoid accidents.

Scenario #93. Smart highways also help with travel-related information and route planning.

Table 1.16   Traffic Control by Smart Highways

Traffic Control by Smart Highways	Enabling Intel Technologies
■ Roadside units collect traffic flow and road condition data using sensors and wireless gateway servers. ■ They can share data with in-vehicle systems and regional servers connected through wireless links. ■ Roadside units trigger speed, collision, or weather alerts communicated through in-vehicle infotainment (IVI) systems in smart cars to warn drivers.	■ The data communications and computing infrastructure needs to be scalable, energy-efficient, and high performance. ■ Embedded Intel® Atom™ processors used in roadside unit gateways ■ Embedded Intel Atom processors used in vehicles ■ Embedded Intel® Xeon® processors used in highway management servers

Collision-Avoiding Smart Cars

Table 1.17 describes collision-avoiding smart cars and the corresponding enabling technologies from Intel.

Scenario #94. Smart cars use biometric identification to identify drivers. Smart Cars adjust seat, mirrors, etc personalized to the driver. Smart cars can drive and park themselves. Smart cars have Internet connectivity and keep people productive and entertained with personalized choices of music, audio books, satellite TV, online gaming, and streaming video.

Scenario #95. Smart cars avoid collisions and streamline traffic flow. They can also smooth out traffic jams by constantly sharing data and sending/receiving alerts with smart highways and other smart cars through wireless in-vehicle systems.

Scenario #96. Smart cars drive safely. Speed warning sensors from roadside units trigger alerts to smart cars to warn drivers if their speed is too high while approaching curves. Collision warning sensors from roadside units on intersections trigger alerts to smart cars to warn drivers of the presence of approaching vehicles, bicycles, or pedestrians. Road monitoring sensors from roadside units also send smart cars driver advisories concerning ice, wet pavement, and other weather conditions.

Scenario #97. Smart cars have sensors and they stream real-time data on speed and road conditions to the nearest roadside unit, which analyzes the information for transmission to following vehicles, intelligent road signs, or automated highway advisory radio systems. Smart cars have intelligent awareness that can recognize that a pedestrian is crossing the road ahead. Smart cars use interior cameras to determine if the driver is falling asleep, warn the drivers to brake, or they halt themselves.

Table 1.17   Collision-Avoiding Smart Cars

Collision-Avoiding Smart Cars	Enabling Intel Technologies
■　Smart cars have intelligent vehicle infotainment (IVI) systems on open infotainment platforms (OIPs) and need processors with special abilities. ■　Smart cars use embedded processors, an embedded operating system. They require low power processors and they must be energy efficient. Smart cars require the ability to withstand harsh temperatures and have wireless connectivity. ■　Parallelism for more efficient use of processor resources, higher processing throughput on multithreaded software. ■　Multi-application performance and separation of mission critical and multimedia infotainment applications.	■　OIPs can be based on energy-efficient Intel® Atom™ processors that support embedded operating systems and wireless networking options, including 3G cellular, and Wi-Fi. ■　Intel Atom processor Z5xx works in the -40° to 85° C temperature range. ■　Embedded Intel® architecture platforms have low power consumption. ■　Intel® Hyper-Threading Technology enables thread-level parallelism and uses processor resources efficiently. ■　Intel® Virtualization provides separation between applications.

Cargo Management by Smart Railcars

Table 1.18 describes cargo managing smart rail cars and the corresponding enabling technologies from Intel.

Scenario #98. Railcars help manage the cargo they carry. Wireless sensor networks consisting of smart, embedded radio frequency identification (RFID) sensors monitor railcars in real time. They can report on the location of each railcar, its operating condition, or parameters affecting the cargo, and help track the progress of freight shipments in real time. Railroad personnel have handheld devices with which they can check on conditions within each car regarding onboard storage.

Scenario #99. Railways accidents like derailments are prevented. Mounted within the rails, a smart wireless sensor network captures real-time data that measures the vibration and temperature of wheel bearings to predict failure before it occurs. Railcars send alerts when maintenance of any kind is required.

Scenario #100. Wirelessly connected radio frequency identification (RFID) sensors on rail cars help track the progress of freight shipments in real time.

Scenario #101. Self-configuring wireless sensor networks within the rail cars capture real-time data that measures the vibration and temperature of wheel bearings to predict failure before it occurs.

Table 1.18   Cargo Managing Smart Railcars

Cargo Managing Smart Railcars	Enabling Intel Technologies
■ Wireless sensors deployed on railcars detect temperature, humidity fluctuations, mechanical shock, and the security of the car and its contents. ■ Sensors use proximity detection data for anti-collision and automatic braking systems. ■ Wireless sensor networks provide distributed sensing of physical conditions in real time, based on mesh network technology. ■ Wireless sensor networks connect via an IEEE 802.15.4 protocol with an embedded router device. ■ The embedded router device does intra-car data processing and storage, network and power management, and routes secure inter-car communications. ■ A powered gateway server located in the locomotive runs Web services applications, performs network management of the inter-car mesh network created by the railcar routers, manage database storage and integrate with external enterprise systems using a wide area network technologies.	■ Ultra-low power embedded Intel® Atom™ processor with power efficiency algorithms and power harvesting capabilities. ■ The tiny wireless sensors are partially powered by the vibration of the car itself using power harvesting. Each sensor can operate on as little as 20 milliamps of electrical current. ■ Embedded multi-core Intel processors that support real-time and open source operating systems for management of the wireless sensor network, data collection and communication. ■ Each router is a multi-protocol wireless computing platform with an Intel Atom processor, memory, storage, I/O, and radio components optimized for long life and low power. ■ These on-railcar devices also communicate via Wi-Fi with handheld mobile devices that enable railroad personnel to query historical data from onboard storage.

Personalized Guidance by Smart Signs

Table 1.19 describes smart signs and the corresponding enabling technologies from Intel.

Scenario #102. Remotely controlled signboards display messages in text and video that are relevant for your journey. For example: discounted deals or weather information for your specific destination is displayed on a real-time basis to signboards around you.

Scenario #103. The smart signs around you "know" you, where you are going, what your tastes and habits are, and display timely and targeted messages for you. They show you images of attractions; promote restaurants, entertainment, spa services, hotels, and other features. You can even play games on these screens that use cell phones as controllers.

Table 1.19   Smart Signs

Smart Signs	Enabling Intel Technologies
■ Signage appliances are used to send timely and targeted messages. ■ A smart digital signage system is managed and controlled remotely using a server system that runs across a LAN, Wi-Fi and the local cellular network. ■ Software features enable travelers to interact with the signs dynamically.	■ Signage appliances can use the Intel® Core™2 Duo mobile processor P8400 and mobile Intel® GM45 Express Chipset. ■ This platform provides very high performance at low power consumption enabling fanless operation. ■ The integrated graphics capability and performance quality is strong enough to meet high-definition video broadcasting requirements.

In intelligent transportation environments, vehicles carry computing and communication platforms, and have enhanced sensing capabilities. Smart sensors have embedded microprocessors and wireless communication.

Vehicle communication technologies are the key to intelligent transportation, since such technologies efficiently improve the transport quality and provides for road safety and security, traffic monitoring, and driving comfort.

Intelligent Vehicle Ad Hoc Network (InVANET) is a specialized form of mobile ad-hoc networks. A special electronic device is placed inside each vehicle that provides ad-hoc network connectivity for the passengers. InVANET enables definition of safety measures in vehicles, streaming communication between vehicles, infotainment and telematics. Other wireless technologies for intelligent transportation are dedicated short range communications (DSRC), cellular communications, and satellite communications.

This area presents many computing and communication challenges for network management, due to the extremely dynamic network topology and the large variable number of mobile nodes:

- Radio channel challenges:
  o Numerous hops of packets degrades strength and quality of signal
  o Extreme mobility of nodes fades the signal
  o Decentralization challenges:
  o Self organizing networks do not ensure optimal bandwidth usage
  o The transmission events are not synchronized and packet collisions occur
- Mobility challenges
  o Mobility of cars make predefined routings meaningless
  o Discovery of time-sensitive and location-based services
  o Challenges of vehicles and service providers discovering each other
- Computing challenges:
  o A distributed computing framework needed to analyze data sent by systems with densely instrumented arrays of sensors
  o Central collection and processing of data does not scale

o Security and privacy challenges

o Contextual information critical, but sharing of context contradicts privacy

o Communication paradigm needed

o For collection, management, and provision of context-aware information on traffic and current location.

More Intelligent Environments of the Future

Intelligent environments of the future might include:

- Autonomous systems and ambient intelligence
- Autonomic and distributed mechatronic and embedded systems
- Bio-mechatronics and bio-sensors
- Cyber-physical systems and cooperative systems
- Embedded computer vision
- Diagnosis and monitoring in mechatronic systems
- Mechatronic and embedded system applications
- Mechatronic and embedded systems for renewable energy systems
- Mechatronic control and electrical vehicular systems
- Robotics and mobile machines
- Sensors and micro electro mechanical systems (MEMS)
- Sensor networks and networked embedded systems
- Small unmanned aerial vehicle technologies and applications

Intelligent Environmental Monitoring

Many scenarios described above use wireless sensors. This section highlights how the wireless sensors enable environmental monitoring in different scenarios.

A wireless sensor network is a wireless network consisting of spatially distributed autonomous miniaturized devices using wireless sensors to cooperatively monitor physical or environmental conditions at different locations.

Each node in the network is an autonomous unit consisting of four functional units: sensor for sensing, embedded microprocessors for data processing, radio transceivers for wireless communications, and a battery unit for power. These nodes are low power, low cost and multifunctional.

All these field-scattered sensor nodes collect data from the field. They then route the real-time data packets through the multi-hop network structure to a base station or a sink. The base station performs fusion so as to eliminate redundancy.

Wireless sensor networks are mesh networks that are ad hoc, multi-hop, self-configuring, self-healing, and capable of dynamic routing and offer a pervasive, fine-grained network.

The networking protocols used are: IEEE 802.15.4 standard for physical and MAC (Medium Access Layer) layers, ZigBee standard for network and application layer, and IEEE 1451 standard for Smart Transducer Interfaces for connecting sensors and actuators.

Scenario #104. Most physical or environmental conditions are monitored, managed and controlled in real time by wireless sensor networks by a collection of small, intelligent, connected sensor distributed in space. Collectively the wireless sensor networks monitor temperature, light, sound, vibration, pressure, humidity, pollutants, soil composition, and object attributes like size, weight, speed, and direction.

Scenario #105. Wireless sensors are sprayed everywhere where wired devices cannot be deployed. For example: inhospitable terrains, battlefields, outer space, deep oceans, glaciers, forests, mountains, wildlife monitoring.

Scenario #106. Most environmental threats like flood and volcanoes are forecast based on observations by wireless sensor networks.

Scenario #107. Structures like building and bridges are monitored by wireless sensor networks to observe vibration, acoustic emissions, and response to stimuli to detect any distress in structures.

Scenario #108. Smart rails, smart highways, smart lights, and so on apply intelligence to real-time data, all using wireless sensor networks. Wireless sensor networks interact with smart cars to provide them route and other navigation related guidance based on real-time demand and availability of smart roads.

Scenario #109. Wireless sensor networks help manage fleets of transportation vehicles (cars, vans, trucks, trains) in real time, in functions such as vehicle maintenance, vehicle tracking, vehicle diagnostics, vehicle route assignment management, fuel management, health and safety management.

Scenario #110. Wireless sensor networks are used in precision agriculture for fertilizer and humidity sensing in farms, and monitoring of environmental conditions that affect irrigation.

Scenario #111. Wireless sensor networks are used in telematics for roads and traffic management.

Scenario #112. Wireless sensor networks are used in intelligent buildings to monitor climate and adjust the climate controls accordingly.

Scenario #113. Wireless sensor networks are used for robot control and guidance in autonomous environments.

Scenario #114. Even human beings are monitored by wireless sensor networks; sensors are worn close to the body. They can detect acceleration in heart rate or an elderly person living alone who falls down the stairs.

Scenario #115. Real-time environmental monitoring enables forecasting. Real-time data is gathered from environmental sensors, such as the size and number of automobiles on the road, weather conditions, and final destinations. Current demands are analyzed and future demand forecasts are made.

Scenario #116. We are in touch with environment all the time: There are sensors everywhere that sense environment, on roads, ocean floors, homes, offices, and so on. The sensors also monitor and report, using associated actuators, any unusual or undesirable trends.

Scenario #117. Wireless sensor networks are used in environmental monitoring to track the movement of birds and insects, detection of forest fires or floods, and pollution.

Scenario #118. The sensors are in the fabric of building, infrastructure, and clothing to monitor and report unusual or undesirable trend, say irregular heartbeat, major pothole on roadway, or a fire.

Scenario #119. Emergency response is activated automatically. Climate and earthquake sensors inform residents of faraway towns of danger.

Scenario #120. Embedded systems analyze the moisture and nitrogen levels in plants and alert operators in case they need to be watered or fertilized.

The unique features of wireless sensor networks bring unique challenges. Some of these features are: unattended operations, short range broadcast, multi hop routing, and dense deployment, cooperative effort of sensor nodes, frequently changing topology, limitations of energy, memory and computing ability. Listed below are some of the challenges we need to overcome:

- Data transfer challenges:
  o Data redundancy due to cooperative nature of network
  o Unreliable due to packet loss in case of congested nodes
  o Latency causes loss of data freshness
  o Data integrity compromised by malicious removal of fragments
  o Density of nodes makes it hard to manage global identification of nodes
- Network challenges
  o Spoofed routing information causes routing loops, attraction or repulsion of network traffic, fake error messages, increase node to node latency
  o Selective forwarding by malicious or malfunctioning nodes
- Availability challenges:
  o Constraints of energy cause frequent fading or failure of nodes.
  o Unreliable communications channel
  o Network management challenge due to frequent topology changes
- Security challenges:

o Constrained resources consumed for implementing security functions, such as encrypt, decrypt, and cryptographic key management

o Unattended deployment in remote environments leave network open to physical attacks, thus requiring special tamperproof packaging

o Ad-hocism and auto-configuration in network makes it difficult to establish trust relationship with key management.

o Susceptible to Denial of Service attacks with simple channel saturation caused by blocking by malicious more powerful nodes

o Traffic analysis attacks can easily identify base station by generation of monitored events or following direction of packets

Radio Frequency Identification (RFID) of Smart Things

In the Internet of Things concept of computing and communicating, everything is a smart thing, Internet enabled and connected to other smart things. That includes all everyday objects around us like cars, cups, refrigerators, lights, and toasters. These objects are the endpoints of the network or the edge of the Web.

These connected countless things can communicate with each other in the form of web services and data exchange. The things are smart enough to adapt to changing situations without human intervention.

The environment is intelligent due to these smart things. Smart things are the building block of the Internet of Things. These smart things react autonomously to the real world.

All physical objects are linked to online world. All physical things have a map in the virtual world, along with temporal and spatial data, which is shaped by the characteristic of the wireless sensor networks used to access the physical object.

All business processes like manufacturing, distribution, management, and recycling all are automated by use of smart things that understand and react to their environment.

The Internet of Things collaborates with wireless sensor networks, which communicate additional information using sensors to record information of the object as well as its environment. The wireless sensor networks and the Internet of Things can communicate with each other using standard protocols.

RFID enables quick identification of items, and is based on radio waves. RFID has three functional components: the RFID tag, the interrogator, and the backend system.

RFID can be read even if the interrogator is not within line of sight. RFID tags also have some memory to write data upon. Most RFID tags have an identifier, stored in nonvolatile memory, thus RFID tags need not be powered all the time to store that identifier. However, power is harvested from the interrogator signal so the tag can operate. RFID tags can have various stages of being active (or totally passive) depending on energy available and the application requirements.

Scenario #121. Electronic article surveillance is done in shops to prevent theft. Alarms go off when an activated RFID tag goes through the gates. Hospitals use it to track patients and their medicines and supplies.

Scenario #122. Every object is identified by a unique address. Every thing is equipped with smart RFID chips with which the objects are identified.

Scenario #123. All physical objects tagged have an RFID transponder and can report information about location, identity, and history over wireless connections. With a associated sensors they can even report information about their environment.

Scenario #124. The physical and the virtual world have been integrated. RFID has enabled association of each globally accessible virtual object accompanying each physical object that contains both current and historical information on that object's physical properties, origin, ownership and sensory context. Such information is available in real time, from anywhere.

Scenario #125. All household objects can be identified and configured remotely.

Scenario #126. Countless intelligent RFIDs will report their location, identity, and history over wireless connection.

Scenario #127. Everything is managed by computer. Nothing is wasted. Nothing will be out of stock.

Scenario #128. Assets are monitoring and identified. Animals are tracked. Pets can be located and tracked.

Scenario #129. Centralized control of intelligent household objects are customized for the owner.

In the Internet of Things, smart things and services associated with them can appear and disappear from the network anytime. Thus there is a need for applications to interface with these services. The applications expect the objects to respond in a manner that changes along with the context. For example: a smart thing may be expected to be in either monitoring mode or alert mode, depending on the application requirement.

Any devices can interconnect with any device, thus naming, addressing, search and discovery of smart things is a challenge that needs addressing.

The Internet of Things changes a physical object into a smart thing where it is open to malicious attack from anywhere in the Internet.

Some of the challenges in developing the Internet of Things include:

- RFID challenges:
  - o Reduction of tag sizes: so even the smallest thing is on the Internet of Things.
  - o Increase in range where RFID can be read for greater application flexibility.
- Power challenges:
  - o RFID tags that use active power cannot operate once onboard power runs out
  - o Power leakages when RFID tags are sleeping
  - o Low Power Wireless – 6LoWPAN
- Security challenges:

    o Smart things can be attacked from anywhere, physical proximity not needed

    o Performance and quality of service management challenges

- Network configuration challenges
- Scalability challenges
- Addressability challenges
- IPv6 size address space needed: 2^{28}
- Adaptive, secure, and pervasive requirement of the Internet of Things presents challenges in systems, architectures, communications protocols, middleware and application support, data processing, search capabilities, and low power technologies
- Challenges of integration with wireless sensor networks so both identification and monitoring can be done.

       This is but a partial list of opportunities for all of us that lie ahead. Well over one hundred such scenarios are listed; there could be many, many more.

       These scenarios describe how life within intelligent environments will look and feel like in the future. It also discusses the challenges that need to be addressed for us to get there, and some of the enabling Intel technologies.

2

Intel Core Technologies for Intelligent Environments

I ntelligent environments need scalable, low power, high performing, and small form factor technologies. Intel® architecture, with its processors, systems on a chip, and advanced technologies, provides the necessary hardware building blocks for intelligent environments. Intel architectures have demonstrated four decades of continuous innovation, while providing a stable, backwardly compatible computing platform.

Introduction

The latest generation of Intel processors provides embedded solutions with high performance, low power multi core processors in a small form factor. The Intel® Atom™ processor is Intel's smallest processor built with the world's smallest transistors and manufactured on Intel's industry-leading 45nm high-k metal gate technology.

Intel's System-On-Chip (SoC), like the technologies codenamed Tolapai and Tunnel Creek, provide an integrated processer for embedded applications. These integrated processor chips eliminate the need for a large number of different chips for different functionality.

Intel advanced technologies built into Intel processors, chipsets, and I/O devices enhance the security, efficiency, and manageability of embedded systems in intelligent environments. These technologies include Intel Hyper Threading Technology, Intel Turbo Boost Technology, and Intel Trusted Execution Technology.

Intel architecture has shown upward compatibility over the years and new innovations have overcome the limitations of earlier processors, as illustrated in Table 2.1. All Intel processors, starting from the 8086 processor of 1978 to the Intel® Core™ i7 processors of 2007, are based on Intel architecture. The very same object code of three decades still executes today on the latest Intel processors.

Table 2.1   Intel® Architecture Evolution

Number of instructions	Years	Instruction Set
100s	1970s	8086, 8088
200s	1980s	80386
300s	1990s	80486
400–600s	2000s	Intel® Supplemental Streaming SIMD Extensions (Intel SSE, SSE2, SSE4)
700s	2010s	Intel® Advanced Encryption Standard - New Instructions (Intel AES-NI)

Intel® Architecture Building Blocks

The basic components of the Intel architecture system are the CPU, memory controller hub (MCH), and I/O controller (ICH). The interfaces are:

• FSB – Front Side Bus
• Intel® QPI – Intel Quick Path Interconnect
• DMI – Direct Media Interface
• High Speed I/O Controller

The basic flow of information in an Intel architecture system utilizes the memory and I/O controller. During the power-on or reset of the system, the BIOS firmware configures the memory and I/O controllers as to where in the CPU's memory map they will reside.
In the Intel architecture system:

• The CPU can control the flow of data, or I/O devices can directly transfer data to and from system memory, or in some cases directly between I/O devices.

- The CPU can use the data from the external devices that was placed in memory, or it can directly transfer data to and from I/O and memory.
- The CPU can also directly access I/O without using memory.
- The CPU is able to do both memory and I/O operations, and these operations apply to two separate address ranges throughout the Intel architecture system.

Intel 64 Architecture

Intel 64 architecture delivers 64-bit computing on server, workstation, desktop and mobile platforms when combined with supporting software. Intel 64 architecture improves performance of all earlier processors in following ways:

- Addressing more than 4 GB of both virtual and physical memory.
- Supporting 64-bit computing: 64-bit flat virtual address space, 64-bit pointers, 64-bit wide general purpose registers, and 64-bit integer support.
- Providing up to one terabyte (TB) of platform address space.
- 8 additional general-purpose registers (GPRs)
- 8 additional registers for streaming SIMD extensions
- Uniform byte-register addressing
- Fast interrupt-prioritization mechanism
- A new instruction-pointer relative-addressing mode

The technology also introduces a new operating mode referred to as IA-32e mode. IA-32e mode operates in one of following two sub-modes:

- compatibility mode enables a 64-bit operating system to run most legacy 32-bit software unmodified,
- 64-bit mode enables a 64-bit operating system to run applications written to access 64-bit address space.

An Intel 64 architecture processor supports existing IA-32 software because it is able to run all non-64-bit legacy modes supported by IA-32 architecture. Most existing IA-32 applications also run in compatibility mode.

Intel Microarchitectures

The following microarchitectures bring relevant features for the enablement of Intelligent Environments.

Intel® Core™ Microarchitecture

Intel® Core™ microarchitecture has multiple features that enable high performance and power-efficient performance for single-threaded as well as multithreaded workloads:

- Intel® Advanced Smart Cache comprises a large on-die shared last level cache that reduces latency to data, improving performance and power efficiency. Intel Advanced Smart Cache delivers higher bandwidth from the second level cache to the core, and optimal performance and flexibility for single threaded and multi-threaded applications.
- Intel® Smart Memory Access prefetches data from memory in response to data access patterns and reduces cache-miss exposure of out-of-order execution.
- Intel® Advanced Digital Media Boost improves most 128-bit SIMD instruction with single-cycle throughput and floating-point operations.

Intel® Atom™ Microarchitecture

Intel Atom microarchitecture maximizes power-efficient performance for single threaded and multi-threaded workloads by providing:

- Advanced micro-ops execution
- Intel® Smart Cache
- Efficient memory access
- Intel® Digital Media Boost

Intel® Microarchitecture Codename Nehalem

Intel microarchitecture codename Nehalem provides the foundation for many innovative features of Intel Core i7 processors. It builds on the success of 45-nm Intel Process Technology.

Intel Core microarchitecture and provides the following feature enhancements:

- Enhanced processor core
- Intel Smart Memory Access
- Intel® Hyper-Threading Technology
- Dedicated Power management Innovations

Intel® Atom™ Architecture

The Intel Atom architecture includes Intel products designed to operate in the industrial (or extended) temperature range: -40 to +85 degrees

C. This makes them suitable for use in intelligent environments that extend to harsh temperature conditions.

Intel Atom architecture utilized the same basic data flows as earlier Intel architecture, but instead of the MCH and ICH, the Intel Atom processor can connect to a Intel® System Controller Hub (Intel SCH).

The Intel SCH integrates most of the MCH and ICH functionality into one device that optimizes the interfaces for ultra low power applications. The Intel SCH provides a similar power management role as the ICH and should be powered first.

The different I/O and peripheral interfaces are:

- SDIO: Secure digital Input/output used for media cards.
- MMC: Multimedia card used for media cards.
- SDVO: Serial digital video out used for display interface.
- LVDS: Low voltage digital signaling used for flat panel display interface.

The Intel Atom processor design is optimized for very low power consumption. The voltage levels are lower and the speed of the FSB is lower. The lower speed FSB allows CMOS drivers to be used, which draw lower power. Another capability of the Intel Atom CPU is to dynamically reduce chip cache size to save power. The Intel SCH has many advanced power management capabilities to enable the lowest possible platform power consumption.

System Memory Control

The Intel SCH integrates a single channel DDR2 system memory controller with a single, 64-bit wide interface.

PCI Express (PCIe) Interface

The Intel SCH contains two PCI Express expansion interfaces. Its high bandwidth, low pin-count serial interface is ideal for I/O expansion.

Parallel ATA (PATA) interface

Parallel ATA (PATA) is an interface standard for the connection of storage devices such as hard disks, solid-state drives, and CD-ROM drives.

Intel High Definition Audio

This link from Intel SCH allows a maximum of two codecs to be connected.

USB interface

The Intel SCH supports a maximum of eight USB ports.

I/O Advanced Programmable Interrupt Controller

The Intel SCH supports I/O APIC specification where PCI devices deliver interrupts as write cycles that are written directly to a register that represents the desired interrupt.

RTC- Real-Time Clock

The Intel SCH contains a real-time clock (RTC) with 256 bytes of battery-backed static RAM. The internal RTC module provides two key functions: keeping date and time and storing system data in its RAM when the system is powered down.

Intel Processors for Embedded Applications

There are various Intel processors that can be used in embedded application. The smallest form factor is the Atom family of processors.

Intel® Atom™ Processor Overview

Intel Atom's distinguishing features enable it for intelligent environments. The Intel Atom processor brings Intel architecture to a small form factor, and as a result, it can work in thermally constrained fanless embedded applications. Intel Atom brings robust performance per watt in a 13 x 14 mm package. The Intel System Controller Hub that goes with Intel Atom processor is in a 22 x 22 mm package. Both together consume less than 5W. Industrial automation is applied typically in a harsh operating environment. Intel 45 nm technologies reduce power consumption, increase switching speed, and increase transistor density over earlier 65 nm technology. The Intel Atom processor is designed for low power embedded applications.

While the Intel Atom processor is currently prevalent in netbooks (with the platform codenamed Menlow), the new platform codenamed Moorestown shrinks and integrates more functions into fewer chips so that it can slip into mobile Internet devices (MIDs) and larger smart phones. It also adds hyper-threading to Intel Atom, boosting performance in threaded applications. Intel has reduced power consumption (especially idle power). Moorestown is built on a 45-nm process; Intel 32-nm chips codenamed

Medfield will further integrate parts of the whole platform into a single piece of silicon and continue to reduce size and power consumption.

The Intel Atom processors are built on 45 nm process technology. They are based on a new microarchitecture, Intel Atom microarchitecture, which is optimized for ultra low power devices. The Intel Atom microarchitecture features two in-order execution pipelines that minimize power consumption, increase battery life, and enable ultra-small form factors. It provides the following features:

- Enhanced Intel SpeedStep Technology
- Intel® Hyper-Threading Technology
- Deep Power Down Technology with Dynamic Cache Sizing
- Support for new instructions up to and including Intel® Supplemental Streaming SIMD Extensions 3 (Intel SSSE3).
- Support for Intel® Virtualization Technology
- Support for Intel 64 Architecture

Intel® Atom™ Processors

Table 2.2 summarizes the features of the Intel Atom processor family.

Table 2.2   Intel® Atom™ Processors (Intel 64)

Intel® Atom™ Processor	Intel® Atom™ Processor 330
Intel Atom microarchitecture	Intel Atom microarchitecture
Intel 64 architecture	Intel 64 architecture
	Dual core
Intel® Virtualization Technology	Intel® Virtualization Technology
Frequency: 2.0–1.60 GHz	Frequency: 1.60 GHz
Maximum external address space: 64 GB	Maximum external address space: 64 GB
On-die caches: L1= 56 KB; L2 = 512 KB	On-die caches: L1 = 56 KB; L2 = 512 KB

Intel® Atom™ Processor D410 (Intel Atom D410 Desktop Processor for Embedded Computing)

The single-core Intel Atom processor N410, based on Intel 45nm process technology, features integrated graphics and memory controllers for robust performance. Intel Embedded Flexible Design enables scalability for the first time on Intel Atom processors.

Intel® Atom™ Processor N450 (Intel Atom N450 Mobile Processors for Embedded Computing)

Based on Intel 45nm process technology, the Intel Atom processor N450 features single-core processing and Enhanced Intel Deeper Sleep (C4/C4E), which reduces power consumption while the processor is idle.

Intel® Atom™ Processor D510 (Intel Atom D510 Desktop Processor for Embedded Computing)

Based on Intel 45nm process technology, the Intel Atom processor N510 features dual-core processing, which performs full parallel execution of multiple software threads to enable higher levels of performance over the previous-generation Intel Atom processor N270.

Intel® Core™ i7 Processors

Table 2.3 summarizes the features of the Intel Core i7 processor family.

Table 2.3   Intel® Core™ i7 Processors (Intel 64)

Intel® Core™ i7-620M Processor	Intel® Core™ i7-965 Processor Extreme Edition
Intel microarchitecture codename Westmere	Intel microarchitecture codename Nehalem
Dual core	Quad core
Intel® Turbo Boost Technology	Intel® QuickPath Interconnect (Intel QPI)
Intel® Hyper-Threading Technology	Intel® Hyper Threading Technology
Intel 64 architecture	Intel 64 architecture
Intel® Virtualization Technology	Intel® Virtualization Technology
Integrated graphics	
Frequency: 2.66 GHz	Frequency: 3.20 GHz
Maximum external address space: 64 GB	Maximum external address space: 64 GB
On-die caches: L1 = 64 KB; L2 = 256 KB	On-die caches: L1 = 64 KB; L2 = 256 KB; L3 = 8 MB

Intel® Core™ i7 (Intel Core i7 Desktop Processors for Embedded Computing)

Based on Intel 45nm process technology, the Intel Core i7 processor features quad-core processing and intelligent performance capabilities, such as

Intel Turbo Boost Technology and Intel Hyper-Threading Technology for demanding embedded applications.

Intel® Core™ i7 (Intel Core i7 Mobile Processors for Embedded Computing)

Based on 32nm process technology, dual-core Intel Core i7 processors feature intelligent performance, power efficiency, integrated graphics, and error correcting code (ECC) memory on industry-standard x86 architectures.

The Intel Core i7 processor 900 series support Intel 64 architecture. They are based on Intel microarchitecture codename Nehalem using 45 nm process technology.

The Intel Core i7 processor includes the following innovative features:

• Intel Turbo Boost Technology converts thermal headroom into higher performance.
• Intel Hyper-Threading Technology in conjunction with quad core to provide four cores and eight threads.
• Dedicated power control unit to reduce active and idle power consumption.
• Integrated memory controller on the processor supporting three channel of DDR3 memory.
• 8 MB inclusive Intel Smart Cache
• Intel Quick Path Interconnect (Intel QPI) providing point-to-point link to chipset.
• Support for SSE4.2 and SSE4.1 instruction sets.
• Second generation Intel Virtualization Technology.

Intel® Xeon® Processors

Table 2.4 summarizes the features of the Intel Xeon processor family.

Table 2.4   Intel® Xeon® Processor 7000 Series (Intel 64)

Intel® Xeon® Processor 7560	Intel® Xeon® Processor 7460
Intel microarchitecture codename Nehalem	Enhanced Intel® Core™ microarchitecture
Eight cores	Six cores
Intel® Turbo Boost Technology	
Intel® Hyper-Threading Technology	
Intel 64 architecture	Intel 64 architecture
Intel® Virtualization Technology	Intel® Virtualization Technology
Integrated graphics	
Frequency: 2.26 GHz	Frequency: 2.67 GHz
Maximum external address space: 16 TB	Maximum extern address space: 1024 GB
On-die caches: L1 = 64 KB; L2 = 256 KB; L3 = 24 MB	On-die caches: L1 = 64 KB; L2 = 3 MB; L3 = 16 MB

The Intel Xeon processor 7500 and 6500 series are based on Intel microarchitecture codename Nehalem using 45 nm process technologies. They support the following innovative features:

- Up to eight cores per physical processor package.
- Up to 24 MB inclusive Intel Smart Cache.
- Provides Intel Scalable Memory Interconnect (Intel SMI) channels
- 7500 Scalable Memory Buffer to connect to system memory.
- Advanced RAS supporting software recoverable machine check architecture.

Intel System on Chip (SoC) for Embedded Applications

SoCs are integrated processor chips that integrate many components used along with a processor into a single integrated circuit chip. SoCs may integrate on a single chip the following:

- Processor
- I/O controllers
- Memory controllers
- Security functions
- Sensor and actuator functionality

- Data and signal processing
- Communication functions

Such single chip SoCs can be used in the computing end points of intelligent environments.

Intel's two SoCs that can be used in building intelligent environments, codenamed Tolapai and Tunnel Creek, are discussed here.

Tolapai

Tolapai is the code name of Intel's first system-on-a-chip (SoC) embedded processor. Tolapai is based on the Intel EP80579 Integrated Processor and has a maximum thermal design power (TDP) as low as 11 W.

Based on Intel architecture, the Intel EP80579 Integrated Processor product line is the first in a series of breakthrough system on-a-chip (SOC) processors, delivering excellent performance-per-watt for small form factor designs.

Tolapai is an integrated system on a chip. The SOC consists of:

- Intel architecture–based communications processors
- Memory controller hub (IMCH)
- I/O architecture controller hub (IICH)
- High speed I/O interfaces including PCI Express (PCIe) and Gigabit Ethernet.

Tolapai features high-performance packet processing and security capabilities. The Tolapai architecture provides processing performance, stringent power usage, maintaining Intel architecture implementation and providing the required I/O throughput.

Tolapai processor features:

- CPU runs at 600 MHz–1.2 GHz clock
- Has 256 KB 2-way level 2 cache

Tolapai memory controller IMCH provides the main path to memory for the IA-32 core and all peripherals that perform coherent I/O (such as PCI Express, the IICH to coherent memory). IMCH features include:

- Four channel DMA engine
- PCI Express root complex with 1x8, 2x4, or 2x1 interfaces.
- Operates at 200–400 MHz
- Single channel, 64-bit (and 32-bt) with ECC memory controller for external DDR-2 memory (400–800 MHz).

Tolapai I/O controller IICH provides a set of PC platform-compatible I/O devices that include:
- Two SATA1.0/2.0
- One USB1.1/2.0 host controller supporting two USB ports
- Two serial 16550 compatible UART interfaces.

The Tolapai Acceleration and I/O Complex (AIOC) supports:
- Three Gigabit Ethernet media access controllers
- MDIO
- Local Expansion Bus (LEB)
- Two Controller Area Network (CAN) interfaces
- IEEE1588 (2-GbE and 2-CAN ports)

Tunnel Creek

Tunnel Creek is Intel's low power integrated processor with PCIe as the interface to the different I/O hubs. Utilizing PCIe will enable multiple market-specific IOHs from multiple vendors to be used to scale into a large variety of embedded market segments.

TunnelCreek is the first SoC for embedded systems based on the Intel Atom.

The Tunnel Creek processor is the "mini-SoC" Intel architecture CPU for the small form factor ultra low power embedded segments based on a new architecture partitioning. The new architecture partitioning integrates the 3D graphics engine, memory controller, and other blocks with the Intel architecture CPU core. The processor's PCI Express v1.0 interface allows it to be paired with customer-defined IOH, ASIC, FPGA, and off-the-shelf discrete components. This flexibility in I/O solutions enables embedded applications in which I/O differs from one application to another.

This flexibility in adapting to any kind of application is a key for building intelligent environments including those in areas of telecommunications, digital surveillance, transportation, and digital signage.

Tunnel Creek provides the following all on a single chip:
- Low-power Intel architecture core: with 600 MHz–1.2 GHz clock; On die, 32-KB 4-way L1 instruction cache and 24-KB 6-way L1 data cache; On die, 512-KB, 8-way L2 cache; L2 dynamic cache sizing; 32-bit physical address, 48-bit linear address size support; Intel Streaming SIMD Extension 2 and 3 (Intel SSE2 and Intel SSE3); Supplemental Streaming SIMD Extensions 3 (SSSE3) support.

- System memory controller: supports single-channel DDR2 memory controller with 32-bit data bus.
- PCI Express (four x1 lane) root ports that may be used to attach discrete I/O components or a custom I/O hub for increased I/O expansion.
- LPC interface has three PCI-based clock outputs that may be provided to different I/O devices such as legacy I/O chip.
- Graphics: Tunnel Creek provides an integrated 2D/3D graphic engine that performs pixel shading and vertex shading within a single hardware accelerator.
- Video encoding and video decoding: provides support for MPEG2, MPEG4, VC1, WMV9, H.264 (main and high-profile level 4.0/4.1), and DivX. Tunnel Creek supports MPEG4, H.263, H.264 (baseline@L3), and VGA/QGA.
- Display interfaces: Tunnel Creek supports LVDS and Serial DVO display ports permitting simultaneous independent operation of two displays.
- LVDS interface: Tunnel Creek supports a low-voltage differential signaling interface that allows the graphics and video adapter to communicate directly to an on-board flat panel display.
- Serial DVO (SDVO) display interface: digital display channel capable of driving SDVO adapters that provide interfaces to a variety of external display technologies (such as DVI, TV-Out, and analog CRT).
- Intel High Definition Audio (Intel HD Audio) Controller: A digital interface that can be used to attach different types of codecs (such as audio and modem codecs).
- SMBus Host Controller provides a mechanism for the processor to initiate communications with SMBus peripherals (slaves).
- Serial Peripheral Interface (SPI) supports BIOS boot from SPI flash.
- Power management supporting ACPI specification: a mechanism to allow flexible configuration of various device maintenance routines as well as power management functions including enhanced clock control and low-power state transitions (such as Suspend-to-RAM and Suspend-to-Disk). A hardware-based thermal management circuit permits software independent entrance to low-power states.
- Watchdog Timer (WDT) that can be configured to asserts upon trigger.
- Real-time clock (RTC) provides battery backed-up date and time keeping.
- Supports Intel Virtualization Technology.
- Supports Intel Hyper-Threading Technology.

- Advanced power management features including Enhanced Intel SpeedStep Technology.
- Intel Deep Power Down Technology (C6).

Intel Advanced Technologies for Embedded Applications

Intel technologies for embedded applications include software optimization for multi-core systems, virtualization, system management, application acceleration and more. Built into many Intel processors, chipsets, and I/O devices, these technologies enhance the security, manageability, reliability, flexibility and of embedded systems in intelligent environments.

The Intel® 64 Architectures

Intel 64 architectures provide mechanisms for managing and improving the performance of multiple processors connected to the same system bus. These include:

- Bus locking and/or cache coherency management for performing atomic operations on system memory.
- Serializing of instructions in processors.
- An advance programmable interrupt controller (APIC) located on the processor chip
- A second-level cache is included in the processor package and is tightly coupled to the processor. Processors pins are provided to support an external L2 cache.
- A third-level cache is included in the processor package and is tightly coupled to the processor.

- These multiprocessing mechanisms have the following characteristics:
- Maintain system memory coherency: When multiple processors are attempting simultaneously to access the same address in system memory, some communication mechanism or memory access protocol must be available to promote data coherency and, in some instances, to allow one processor to temporarily lock a memory location.
- Maintain cache consistency: When one processor accesses data cached on another processor, it must not receive incorrect data. If it modifies data, all other processors that access that data must receive the modified data.

- Predictable ordering of writes to memory: In some circumstances, it is important that memory writes be observed externally in precisely the same order as programmed.

- Distribute interrupt handling among a group of processors: When several processors are operating in a system in parallel, it is useful to have a centralized mechanism for receiving interrupts and distributing them to available processors for servicing.

- Increase system performance by exploiting the multi-threaded and multiprocessing nature of contemporary operating systems and applications.

- Intel Streaming SIMD Extensions (SSE) 2 enables software to accelerate data processing in specific areas, such as complex arithmetic and video decoding.

- Intel SSE3, an extension of SSE2, enables software to accelerate data processing by working horizontally in a register, as opposed to the more or less strictly vertical operation of all previous SSE instructions.

- Intel SSE3, an extension of SSE3, contains 16 new discrete instructions over SSE3, enabling software to accelerate data processing.

Intel Power Management Technologies

Intel Power Management Technologies such as Enhanced Intel SpeedStep Technology, Intel Turbo Boost Technology, and Dynamic FSB Frequency Switching help control power consumption through architectural improvements such as integrated power gates and automated low-power states.

Intel processors support a number of power states that enable substantial power savings and are accessible through the industry-standard Advanced Configuration and Power Interface (ACPI).

Power states fall into three categories, as defined below by the ACPI specifications:

- System States (S-states): These states control whether the system is fully on, sleeping with system context saved, in "soft off" or mechanically off.

- Processor States (C-states): C-states manage power consumption at the processor core's TDP (thermal design power) level. Deep sleep (C3) and deeper sleep (C4) are used in the power management by putting the CPU to "sleep" when not in use.

- Performance States (P-states): P-states establish multiple operating points that vary processor frequency and supply voltage.

- These power states allow granular control over the system operation. Some power states save considerable power during periods of low activity and can be used to reduce power consumption.

- Enhanced Intel SpeedStep Technology allows putting a ceiling on the system power consumption. By changing the processor supply voltage and frequency enables optimal performance at the lowest power.

- Intel Turbo Boost Technology establishes a new P-state (highest performance) by increasing the processor frequency above the base operating frequency.

- Dynamic FSB Frequency Switching can be used to reduce the processor front side bus (FSB) frequency to half, thus providing further power savings to P-states.

- Intelligent Intel power management technologies smartly consume only the energy required by the workload. It balances power consumption and system performance for embedded computing systems.

Enhanced Intel SpeedStep Technology (EIST)

Enhanced Intel SpeedStep Technology supports ACPI P-states by providing software interfaces that control the operating frequency and voltage of a processor.

Enhanced Intel SpeedStep Technology provides a way to balance providing higher power when it is needed, and conserving power usage it when not needed.

Enhanced Intel SpeedStep Technology allows the system to dynamically adjust processor voltage and core frequency.

This technology can be used to decrease average power consumption and decrease average heat production that is important for small form factor chips.

Enhanced Intel SpeedStep Technology provides performance and reduces power according to application requirements.

Enhanced Intel SpeedStep Technology works as follows:

- Manage processor power consumption using performance state transitions. These states are defined as discrete operating points associated with different frequencies.

- Centralization of the control mechanism and software interface in the processor by using model-specific registers.

- Reduced hardware overhead; this permits more frequent performance state transitions.

- Separation between voltage and frequency changes. By stepping voltage up and down in small increments separately from frequency changes, the system is able to transition between voltage and frequency states more often

- Clock partitioning and recovery. The bus clock continues running during state transition, even when the core clock and Phase-Locked Loop are stopped, which allows logic to remain active.

Because Enhanced Intel SpeedStep Technology reduces the latency associated with changing the voltage/frequency pair (referred to as P-state), those transitions can be practically undertaken more often, which enables more-granular demand-based switching and the optimization of the power/performance balance based on demand.

Intel® Hyper-Threading Technology (Intel HT Technology)

Intel Hyper-Threading Technology is an extension to Intel 64 and IA-32 architectures that enable a single physical processor to execute multiple threads concurrently.

The performance of applications can be improved by hyper-threading. The working of Intel HT Technology is transparent to the application.

Intel Hyper-Threading Technology enables thread-level parallelism on each processor resulting in more efficient use of processor resources, higher processing throughput, and improved performance on today's multithreaded software.

- Intel HT Technology results in more efficient use of processor resources—higher processing throughput—and improved performance on the multi-threaded software.

- In Intel Hyper-Threading Technology, a single processor core provides two logical processors that share execution resources

- Intel Hyper-Threading Technology improves the performance of IA-32 processors when executing multi-threaded operating system and application code or single-threaded applications under multi-tasking environments.

- The technology enables a single physical processor to execute multiple separate threads concurrently using shared execution resources.

- The benefits of hyper-threading are as: improved support for multi-threaded code, allowing multiple threads to run simultaneously, improved reaction and response time.

- Hyper-threading works by duplicating certain sections of the processor—those that store the architectural state—but not duplicating the main execution resources.
- This allows a hyper-threading processor to appear as two "logical" processors to the host operating system, allowing the operating system to schedule two threads or processes simultaneously.
- When execution resources would not be used by the current task in a processor without hyper-threading, and especially when the processor is stalled, a hyper-threading equipped processor can use those execution resources to execute another scheduled task.
- Intel HT Technology provides hardware multi-threading capability with a single physical package by using shared execution resources in a processor core. It is unlike a multi-processor hardware with multiple physical processors, in that in this case the multiple processors on a single chip are logical.
- This configuration allows multiple threads to be executed simultaneously on each a physical processor.
- Each logical processor executes instructions from an application thread using the resources in the processor core.
- The core executes these threads concurrently, using out-of-order instruction scheduling to maximize the use of execution units during each clock cycle.
- Each logical processor consists of a full set of IA-32 data registers, segment registers, control registers, debug registers, and advanced programmable interrupt controller (APIC).
- At the firmware (BIOS) level, the basic procedures to initialize the logical processors in a processor supporting Intel HT Technology are the same as those for a traditional DP or MP platform. An operating system designed to run on a traditional DP or MP platform may use CPUID to determine the presence of hardware multi-threading support feature and the number of logical processors they provide.

Intel Multi-Core Technology

Intel multi-core technology is an extension to Intel 64 and IA-32 architectures that enable a single physical processor to execute multiple separate code streams concurrently. In Intel multi-core technology, a physical processor package provides multiple processor cores. Both configurations require chipsets and BIOS that support the technologies. Intel multi-core processors have scalable parallel processing performance that enable in space- and power-efficient embedded platforms designs.

- Multi-core technology is another form of hardware multi-threading capability in IA-32 processor families. Multi-core technology enhances hardware multi-threading capability by providing multiple execution cores in a physical package.

- Multi core processors contain multiple CPU or cores in a single physical package. Typical multi-core processors are dual-core, quad-core and eight-core processors.

- Different cores in a multi-core chip are coupled together tightly or loosely depending on the use of shared resources.

- Inter-core communication is done by message passing or shared memory methods.

- Multiple cores can be used to consolidate platforms, run legacy applications, reduce power consumption, increase overall system performance, and share system I/O resources.

- Intel processors can have hardware multi-core support with HT. For example, it can have a dual processor cores as well as Intel Hyper-Threading Technology. This means that the processor has four logical processors in the same physical package two logical processors for each processor core.

- Intel processors can also have hardware multi-threading support with dual processor cores no Intel Hyper-Threading Technology. This means that the processor provides two logical processors in a physical package

Intel® Turbo Boost Technology

Intel Turbo Boost Technology automatically allows processor cores to run faster than the base operating frequency if it's operating below power, current, and temperature specification limits. Thus applications can take advantage of higher speed execution on demand by using available power to run at a higher frequency. It uses the principle of leveraging thermal headroom to dynamically increase processor performance for single-threaded and multi-threaded/multi-tasking environment.

The maximum frequency enabled by Intel Turbo Boost Technology depends on the number of active cores.

The amount of time the processor spends in the Intel Turbo Boost Technology state depends on the workload and operating environment including: Number of active cores, estimated current consumption, estimated power consumption, and the processor temperature.

When the processor is operating below these limits and the user's workload demands additional performance, the processor frequency will dynamically increase by 133 MHz on short and regular intervals until the upper limit is met or the maximum possible upside for the number of active cores is reached.

Intel® Trusted Execution Technology (Intel TXT)

Intel Trusted Execution Technology (Intel TXT) is a set of hardware extensions to Intel processors and chipsets that enhance Intel platforms with security capabilities. These capabilities include measured launch and protected execution. Intel TXT set of capabilities allow critical applications to run in a virtualized, protected environment. They help protect data integrity.

Intel Trusted Execution Technology's hardware-based mechanisms help protect against software-based attacks and protects the confidentiality and integrity of data stored or created on the client PC. It does this by enabling an environment where applications can run within their own space, protected from all other software on the system. These capabilities provide the protection mechanisms, rooted in hardware, that are necessary to provide trust in the application's execution environment. In turn, this can help to protect vital data and processes from being compromised by malicious software running on the platform.

Intel TXT hardware-based security protects memory region provided by domain separation. This memory protection prevents DMA engines from reading or modifying protected memory pages. In contrast, software-based security like firewall, virus scanners, and encryption software can only protect from other malicious software that is running at the same or higher privilege level.

Intel Trusted Execution Technology capabilities include:

- Protected execution and memory spaces where sensitive data can be processed out of view of any other software.
- Sealed storage shields encryption keys and other data from attack while in use or stored.
- Attestation enables a system to provide assurance that it has correctly invoked the Intel Trusted Execution Technology environment, as well as enable a verified measurement of the software running in the protected space.
- Measured launch capability to help verification of platform configuration with a higher level of assurance

- Memory protection enhances protection of system resources, increases confidentiality and integrity of data, improves assurance of data transfers and resources, and improves protection of sensitive information

- Local verification uses the measurement capability of Intel Trusted Execution Technology to allow the local user to have confidence that the platform is executing in a known state. The confidence comes from the hardware ability of Intel Trusted Execution Technology to properly measure the launched configuration and store the measurement in the platform Trusted Platform Module (TPM).

- Remote verification takes the measurements obtained by Intel Trusted Execution Technology and stored in the TPM, and uses the TPM to inform remote (not executing on the platform) entities about the current platform configuration. Of essence in this use model is that the remote entity can rely on the properties of Intel Trusted Execution Technology to provide the protections listed above.

- Multi-level operation takes advantage of the memory protections provided by Intel Trusted Execution Technology to run two or more applications or operating systems that require strict separation and managed communication between the entities. Those wishing to rely on these properties make use of either local or remote verification to ensure that the proper environment is setup and executing.

Intel® Advanced Encryption Standard (AES) New Instructions Technology (AES-NI)

AES (Advanced Encryption Standard) is an block cipher encryption standard widely used to protect network traffic, and data. AES is very widely used in several applications such as network encryption, disk and file encryption applications. File-level and disk encryption applications use AES to protect data stored on a disk. Networking applications use encryption to protect data in flight with protocols encompassing SSL, TLS, IPsec, HTTPS, FTP, SSH, and so on.

Advanced Encryption Standard (AES-NI) new instructions help accelerate secure data encryption and decryption, and improve performance. These instructions accelerate the applications which use Advanced Encryption Standard (AES) block cipher.

There are six instructions that offer full hardware support for AES. Four instructions support the AES encryption and decryption, and other two instructions support the AES key expansion.

The AES instructions have the flexibility to support all usages of AES, including all standard key lengths and standard modes of operation. Their hardware implementations offer a significant increase in performance compared to the current software implementations alone.

Beyond improving performance, the AES instructions provide important security benefits. By running in data-independent time and not using tables, they help in eliminating the major timing and cache-based attacks that threaten table-based software implementations of AES. In addition, they make AES simple to implement, with reduced code size, which helps reducing the risk of inadvertent introduction of security flaws, such as difficult-to-detect side channel leaks. Intel AES-NI implements some of the complex and performance intensive steps of the AES algorithm using hardware and thus accelerating the execution of the AES algorithms.

AES is a symmetric block cipher that encrypts/decrypts data through several rounds. It works by encrypting a fixed block size of 128 bits of plain text in several rounds to produce the final encrypted cipher text.

The number of rounds used depends on the key length. Each round performs a sequence of steps on the input state, which is then fed into the following round. Each round is encrypted using a subkey that is generated using a key schedule.

The new AES-NI instruction set is comprised of six new instructions that perform several compute intensive parts of the AES algorithm. These instructions can execute using significantly less clock cycles than a software solution. Four of the new instructions are for accelerating the encryption/decryption of a round and two new instructions are for round key generation.

The new instructions help address recently discovered side channel attacks on AES. AES-NI instructions perform the decryption and encryption completely in hardware without the need for software lookup tables. Therefore using AES-NI can lower the risk of side-channel attacks as well as greatly improve AES performance.

Intel Thermal Monitoring and Protection Technology

The IA-32 architecture provides the following mechanisms for monitoring temperature and controlling thermal power:
- Catastrophic shutdown detector forces processor execution to stop if the processor's core temperature rises above a preset limit.
- Automatic thermal monitoring thermal monitoring mechanisms force the processor to reduce its power consumption in order to operate within predetermined temperature limits automatically. It has two modes of

operation. One mode modulates the clock duty cycle; the second mode changes the processor's frequency. Both modes are used to control the core temperature of the processor.

- Adaptive thermal monitoring thermal monitoring mechanisms force the processor to reduce its power consumption in order to operate within predetermined temperature limits in an adaptive manner. It can provide flexible thermal management on processors made of multiple cores.

- The software controlled clock modulation mechanism permits operating systems to implement power management policies that reduce power consumption; It modulates the clock duty cycle of the processor. The phrase "duty cycle" refers to the time period during which the clock signal is allowed to drive the processor chip. By using the stop clock mechanism to control how often the processor is clocked, processor power consumption can be modulated.

- On-die digital thermal sensor and interrupt mechanisms permit the OS to manage thermal conditions natively without relying on BIOS or other system board components. It provides access to an on-die digital thermal sensor using a model-specific register and uses an interrupt mechanism to alert software to initiate digital thermal monitoring.

Intel Execute Disable Bit (XD)

Execute disable bit is a hardware-based security feature that can

- prevent harmful software from executing and propagating on the server or network
- help prevent malicious buffer overflow attacks when combined with a supporting operating system
- reduce exposure to viruses and malicious-code attacks
- halt worm attacks
- reduce the need for virus-related repairs
- eliminate the need for software patches aimed at buffer overflow attacks
- when combined with a supporting operating system, stops a worm in its tracks and minimizes data loss and large-scale system infection

Intel Execute Disable Bit can provide valuable security protection, preventing or minimizing costly damage, data loss, and interruption of business operations.

Intel® I/O Acceleration Technology (Intel® I/O AT)

Intel I/OAT is actually a set of technologies that increase performance by enhancing data acceleration across the computing platform:

- Intel® Quick Data Technology enables data copy by the chipset instead of the CPU, to move data more efficiently through the server

- Direct Cache Access (DCA) allows a capable I/O device, such as a network controller, to place data directly into CPU cache thus reducing cache misses

- Extended Message Signaled Interrupts (MSI-X) distributes I/O interrupts to multiple CPUs and cores, for better CPU utilization

- Receive Side Coalescing (RSC) aggregates packets from the same TCP/IP flow into one larger packet, reducing per-packet processing costs for faster TCP/IP processing

- Low latency interrupts tune interrupt interval times depending on the latency sensitivity of the data, using criteria such as port number or packet size

- Intel I/O Acceleration Technologies are Intel platform network technologies that:

- Accelerate, optimize, and seamlessly scale servers with Microsoft Windows Server and Linux operating systems

- Moves data efficiently through networked systems based on Intel multi-core processors

- Acceleration gets network data to applications faster, while optimization allows servers to handle greater loads without increasing power consumption and heat

With Intel I/OAT, servers can handle more networked users and process more data as business needs grow. Plus, systems can process data faster and more efficiently. Users experience better application and network responsiveness with Intel I/OAT.

Intel® Quick Assist Technology

Intel QuickAssist Technology optimizes the use and deployment of accelerators on Intel architecture platforms. It includes a family of interrelated Intel and industry standard technologies and includes a software layer that allows applications to easily manage accelerators.

Intel QuickAssist Technology includes a software layer—the Accelerator Abstraction Layer (AAL)—that allows applications to easily manage accelerators. It also supports acceleration using Intel multi-core processors while leveraging new integrated accelerators inside the Intel processor. As we move to intelligent environments, small form factor accelerators on single processors are greatly needed. Intel QuickAssist Technology will help with the following:

- Field Programmable Gate Array (FSB-FPGA) accelerator hardware modules directly attach to FSB. This accelerates performance due to low latency interconnect.

Intel Quick Assist Technology eliminates the need of proprietary acceleration layers for each new device, thus reducing time to develop.

Intel® Virtualization Technology (Intel® VT)

Intel VT provides hardware-based assistance for virtualization software and enables multiple virtual machines to run on a single system.

Intel VT allows one platform to run multiple operating systems and applications in independent partitions. With virtualization, one computer system can function as multiple "virtual" systems.

Intel VT enables consolidation of servers For example, one single server can function independently both as a business and web server, isolating software loads from possible virus attacks. This also enables creation of virtual "legacy" platforms to run legacy applications, rather than having to keep legacy platforms running.

Intel VT gives the ability to run multiple applications requiring different environments on a single hardware platform. Executing on the same virtualized hardware platform, each application executes within its own OS environment within a separate virtual machine. Virtualization creates a layer of abstraction between underlying physical hardware and the operating system on top.

- The abstraction layer is called the *hypervisor*.
- The hypervisor executes the OS as a guest within a virtual machine environment and virtualizes or emulates the platform resources like CPU, memory, and I/O to the guest OS.
- Multiple guest operating systems can be supported by the hypervisor, each encapsulated within its own virtual machine.
- By abstracting the software away from the underlying hardware, there are many ways to increase efficiency of management of systems, strengthen the security, and make computing infrastructure more resilient in the event of a disaster.

Intel VT has two different components, namely Intel VT-x for support on the processor and Intel VT-d for Directed I/O support in the controller hub.

Intel VT-x constitutes a set of virtual-machine extensions (VMXs) that support virtualization of the processor hardware.

Intel VT-d adds support for I/O-device virtualization to help end users improve security and reliability systems and improve performance of I/O devices in a virtualized environment. Intel VT-d provides IO device assignment to the VM with hardware-assisted DMA and interrupts remapping from the I/O devices.

In intelligent environments, there is a great need to achieve multiple functionalities without multiplying hardware. Virtualization provides that ability.

The challenges associated with this are ensuring security and efficiency as I/O access is done to the virtual machines. Thus penalties of latency need to be addressed. Also, the hypervisor itself comes with an overhead. It is more critical since intelligent environments need real-time latency to work well.

Intel® Active Management Technology (Intel® AMT)

Intel AMT is a hardware-based technology for remotely managing and securing PCs out-of-band. There is a need to run many management and maintenance related functions on systems in intelligent environments remotely. Intel AMT allows services to be run on remote client systems that enable performing of these functions remotely regardless of system state.

- The functions that can be performed remotely by Intel AMT can be device management, provisioning, platform configuration changes, system logs, event management, software inventory, and software and firmware updates.

- Intel AMT enables systems to be monitored, managed, and diagnosed remotely, even if the operating system is not running or the system is powered down or it is not responding.

- Intel AMT manageability can discover failures, proactively alert, event log, remotely heal, recover, and protect networked embedded computing systems from remote.

- Intel AMT Out of Band (OOB) device management allows remote access and management regardless of device power or OS state.

- Devices can be remotely turned on/off to reduce energy consumption during non-peak operating times.

- Intel AMT out-of-band system access allows discovery of assets even while PCs are powered off.

- Intel AMT out-of-band management capabilities allow diagnosing and remote isolation and recovery of systems after OS failures.
- Intel AMT hardware-based agent presence checking proactively checks that software agents are running and detects missing agents
- Intel AMT System Defense proactively blocking incoming threats and isolates infected clients before they impact the network
- Intel AMT remote hardware and software asset tracking updates virus protection across the enterprise
- Intel AMT enables third-party software to store version numbers or policy data in nonvolatile memory for off-hours retrieval or updates.

3

Intel Embedded Platforms for Intelligent Environments

Intel® architecture combines building blocks like processors and SoCs to create platforms. Platforms are a validated combination of an Intel processor and Intel chipset. Intel's newest platforms offer robustness, scalability, low power, and high performance in a small form factor.

Introduction

Intel platforms can be embedded in a variety of intelligent environments, like intelligent hospitals, intelligent transportation, intelligent shopping malls, intelligent surveillance, and intelligent homes.

Intel embedded platforms meet a wide range of constraints of intelligent environments, namely low power, performance and scalability requirement. The platforms below describe how each category meets different type of constraints. Table 3.1 summarizes platform features.

Ultra Low Power Platforms

These platforms include:

- Platforms based on 45 nm technology Intel® Atom™ Z530 processors. They have clock speed up to 1.6 GHz and L2 cache of 512 KB. They have a single core and TDP of 2.2 W.
- Platforms based on 45 nm technology Intel Atom Z510 processors. They have clock speed up to 1.1 GHz and L2 cache of 512 KB. They have a single core and TDP of 2.0 W.

Low Power Platforms

These platforms include:

- Platforms based on 65 nm technology Celeron® M ULV processors. They have clock speed up to 1.06 GHz and L2 cache of 1 MB. They have a single core and TDP of 5.5 W.
- Platforms based on 45 nm technology Intel Atom D510 processors. They have clock speed up to 1.66 GHz and L2 cache of 1 Mb. They have up to 2 cores and TDP of 13 W.
- Platforms based on 45 nm technology Intel Atom D410 processors. They have clock speed up to 1.66 GHz and L2 cache of 512 KB. They have a single core and TDP of 10 W.
- Platforms based on 45 nm technology Intel Atom N450 processors. They have clock speed up to 1.66 GHz and L2 cache of 512 KB. They have a single core and TDP of 5.5 W.
- Platforms based on 32 nm technology Intel® Core™ i7 processors. They have clock speed up to 2.66 GHz and L2 cache of 4 MB. They have up to 2 cores and TDP of 35 W.
- Platforms based on 32 nm technology Intel Core i5 processors. They have clock speed up to 2.4 GHz and L2 cache of 3 MB. They have up to 2 cores and TDP of 35 W.

Performance Platforms

Intel embedded performance platforms include:

- Platforms based 45 nm technologies on Intel® Xeon® series processors have clock speeds up to 2.83 GHz and L2 cache up to 8 MB. They have up to 4 cores and TDP less than 100 W.
- Platforms based on 90 nm technology Intel® EP 80579 Integrated Processor. They have clock speed up to 1.2 GHz and L2 cache of 256 KB. They have TDP less than 25 W.
- Platforms based on 45 nm technology Intel® Core™2 Duo processors. They have clock speed up to 2.53 GHz and L2 cache of 6 MB. They have up to 2 cores and TDP less than 35 W.

Scalable Platforms

Scalable platforms include:

- Platforms based on 45 nm technology Intel Core i7 processors. They have clock speed up to 2.8 GHz and L2 cache of 8 MB. They have up to 4 cores and TDP less than 100 W.

- Platforms based on 45 nm technology Intel Core i5 processors. They have clock speed up to 2.66 GHz and L2 cache of 8 MB. They have up to 4 cores and TDP less than 100 W.
- Platforms based on 32 nm technology Intel Core i5 processors. They have clock speed up to 3.33 GHz and L2 cache of 4 MB. They have up to 2 cores and TDP less than 75 W.
- Platforms based on 32 nm technology Intel Core i3 processors. They have clock speed up to 3.06 GHz and L2 cache of 4 MB. They have up to 2 cores and TDP less than 75 W.

Table 3.1   Intel Embedded Platforms

Platform	Intel Embedded Low Power Entry Platform for 2009 (formerly code named Navy Pier)	Intel Embedded Low Power Small Form Factor SOC Platform for 2008 (formerly code named Tolapai)	Intel Embedded Low Power Small Form Factor Graphics Platform for 2008 (code named Menlow):	Intel Embedded Performance DP Bladed Platform for 2008 (code named Cranberry Lake):
Processor	Intel® Atom™ Processor N270 (512 KB cache, 1.60 GHz, 533 MHz FSB)	Intel® EP80579 Integrated Processor with Intel® QuickAssist Technology, 1066 MHz	Intel® Atom™ Processor Z530 (512 KB cache, 1.60 GHz, 533 MHz FSB)	Intel® Xeon® Processor E5220 (6 MB cache, 2.33 GHz, 1333 MHz FSB)
Chipset	Mobile Intel® 945GSE Express Chipset with 82801GBM I/O Controller Hub (ICH7M)		Intel® SCH US15W Chipset with I/O Controller	Intel® 5100 Chipset with 82801IR I/O Controller Hub (ICH9R)
Platform technologies	Enhanced Intel® SpeedStep® Technology Execute Disable Bit Intel® Hyper-Threading Technology (Intel HT Technology)	Enhanced Intel® SpeedStep® Technology Execute Disable Bit Intel® Hyper-Threading Technology (Intel HT Technology)	Enhanced Intel® SpeedStep® Technology Execute Disable Bit Intel® Hyper-Threading Technology (Intel HT Technology) Intel® Virtualization Technology (Intel VT)	Enhanced Intel® SpeedStep® Technology Execute Disable Bit Intel® 64 architecture Intel® Matrix Storage Technology (Intel MST) Intel® Quiet System Technology (Intel QST) Intel® Virtualization Technology (Intel VT) USB Port Disable feature

Intel Embedded Platforms

Embedded systems based on the Intel Atom processor have the best performance per watt and are very useful for embedded applications. Their Thermal Design Power (TDP) is low—in some configurations, even less than 5 W for the complete platform. The temperature rating range is high, from -40 C to +85 C. This makes Intel Atom–based platforms ideal for embedded applications, which are usually fanless and operate in high ambient temperatures. Here we discuss how we can build simple two-chip solutions for different embedded platforms for intelligent environments with Intel Atom and one more chip.

- A two-chip platform with Intel Atom Z530 and Intel System Controller US 15 W with platform power less than 5 W in small form factor (Menlow)
- A two-chip platform with Intel Atom Z510 and Intel System Controller US 15 W with platform power less than 5 W in large form factor (Menlow XL)
- A two-chip platform with Intel Atom processor N450 along with an Intel 82801HM (ICH8)

Intel Atom is implemented in 45nm process technology and is software compatible with earlier 32-bit Intel architecture.

Intel® Atom™ Z530-based Small Form Factor Graphics Platform (Code Name Menlow)

As discussed, a two-chip platform (Menlow) can be built with the Intel Atom processor by using the Intel Atom Z530 (formerly code named Silverthorne) and Intel System Controller US 15 W (formerly code named Poulsbo). The Intel Atom uses around 2 W and the hub uses around 2 W, both together consume less than 5 W.

This platform utilizes the Intel Atom processor Z530 in small form factor (13x14 mm package) and the Intel System Controller Hub US15W small form factor (22x22 mm package) versions. The platform technologies on this platform are:

- Enhanced Intel SpeedStep Technology
- Execute Disable Bit
- Intel Hyper-Threading Technology (Intel HT Technology)
- Intel Virtualization Technology (Intel VT)

The Intel Atom processor Z530 has ultra low thermal design power (TDP), small form factor, good performance, and the ability to withstand commercial temperature ranges.

The architectural reasons behind these features are as follows:

- Intel Atom is built with Intel's hafnium-based 45-nm Hi-k metal gate silicon technology. This technology reduces power consumption, increases switching speed, and has significantly more transistor density than earlier 65 nm technology.

- Intel Atom combines multiple micro-ops per instruction into a single micro-op and executes in a single cycle. This results in better performance and lesser power consumption.

- Intel Atom has an in-order execution core, which consumes less power than out-of-order execution.

- Intel Atom processor has a new C6 state, which is a "Deep Power Down" state that removes power from processor core and caches.

- Dynamic L2 cache sizing reduces leakage due to transistor sleep mode.

- SSE3 instruction set enables software to accelerate data processing for complex arithmetic and video decoding.

- Intel Atom has CMOS drivers on many of the FSB signals for lower I/O power consumption.

All these hardware features plus advanced power management techniques in Intel Atom are of great need in thermally constrained and fanless embedded applications.

The Intel SCH US 15W is a system controller hub. As discussed above, a two-chip platform can be built with Intel Atom, by using Intel Atom Z5xx series processor and Intel System Controller (SCH US 15W). This combination consumes less than 5 W total platform TDP. Hence it is ideal for many intelligent environments such as can be built in medical, industrial control, and automation areas. Intel SCH US15W combines the Graphics Media Accelerator (Intel GMA 500), memory controller, and I/O controller into a single SCH chip. Key architectural features include:

- Graphics Media Accelerator (Intel GMA 500), a flexible, programmable architecture that supports 2D, 3D and advanced 3D graphics, screen tiling, internal true color processing, zero overhead anti-aliasing, and high-definition video decode, and image processing.

- Dual display pipes with rotation support, along with low-voltage differential signaling (LVDS) and serial DVO (SDVO) display ports, permit simultaneous independent operation of one display or two. SDVO adapters provide interfaces to a variety of external display technologies while the LVDS interface allows the Intel GMA 500 to communicate directly to a flat-panel display.

- Hardware video decode acceleration relieves the decode burden from the processor and reduces power consumption of the system. Full hardware acceleration of H.264, MPEG2, MPEG4, VC1, and WMV9 is supported, eliminating the need for software decode and off-loading the processor.

Intel SCH 15W also has Advanced Configuration and Power Interface (ACPI) management, which exposes platform power management states to the operating system. This enables applications to control system sleep states, device power states, and CPU power states in a power optimizing manner.

Intel® Atom® Z510 based Ultra Low Power Platform (Code Name eMenlow XL)

Ultra low power Intel Atom platforms perform well in low power, fanless, thermally constrained, and small form factor embedded applications. These platforms can handle data from multiple sources over high-bandwidth interconnects. The platform feature specifications are summarized in Table 3.2.

Embedded Menlow XL platform combines the large form factor (22x22 mm package) versions of the Intel Atom Processor Z510 (formerly Silverthorne XL) and the large form factor (37.5x37.5 mm package) versions of the Intel System Controller Hub (formerly Poulsbo XL).

Intel Atom 510 single-core processors are implemented in 45 nm process technology, and are power-optimized so as to provide good performance density.

The processor can be combined with the Intel SCH US15W. This low power SCH has the Intel Graphics Media Accelerator 500, memory controller, and I/O controller.

The Intel SCH US15W provides I/O capabilities including USB 2.0, SDIO and PCI Express†. This platform has a combined TDP under five watts, making it ideal for intelligent environments and smart embedded devices.

Table 3.2	Intel® Atom™ Z510-based Ultra Low Power Platform
Processor	Intel® Atom™ Processor Z510 / Z530
Process	45 nm
Clock speed	1.1 GHz / 1.6 GHz
Platform TDP	4.3 W / 4.5 W
Chipset	US15W
Platform technologies	Enhanced Intel® SpeedStep Technology (EIST) C1E Enhanced Low Power Sleep State Intel Demand Based Switching (IDBS) Execute Disable Bit

Intel® Atom™ N450-based Intensive I/O Computing Platform (Code Name Luna Pier)

This embedded platform pairs the Intel Atom N450 processors with the ICH8. This two chip platform consists of a processor (Intel Atom 450) and a south bridge (ICH8).

On the platform, the Intel Atom processor N450 embedded computing is based on 45 nm process technology with thermal design power (TDP) from 13 W to 5.5W. Also on the platform, the Intel 82801 I/O Controller provides multiple high bandwidth interfaces (PCI Express, PCI, Serial ATA, Hi-Speed USB 2.0) and an Intel High Definition Audio interface. The processor has integrated graphics and memory controllers and can provide graphics core rendering speeds from 200 to 400 MHz while maintaining power efficiency. The DMI Interface between Intel Atom N450 processor and the ICH8 supports 4 lanes in each direction with a signaling rate of 20 Gb/s point-to-point.

The Embedded Intel Atom N450 processors have the following characteristics:

- Consume low power
- Built on 45-nanometer Hi-K process technology
- Single core

Included in Intel Atom N450 processor on a single die are:

- Integrated memory controller (IMC)
- Integrated graphics processing unit (GPU)
- Integrated I/O (IIO)

This embedded platform enables higher performance, lower cost, easier validation, and improved x-y footprint.

System memory supported on the Intel Atom N450 processor–based platform is as follows:

- One channel of DDR2 memory consisting of 64-bit of data lines
- Memory DDR2 data transfer rates of 667 MT/s
- Non-ECC, unbuffered DDR2 SO-DIMMs only
- Maximum of 2-GB memory capacity supported
- Partial writes to memory using Data Mask signals (DM)
- On-die termination (ODT)
- Intel Fast Memory Access (Intel FMA) with just-in-time command scheduling, command overlap and out-of-order scheduling
- Thermal management scheme to selectively manage reads and/or writes. Memory thermal management can be triggered by either on-die thermal sensor, or by preset limits. Management limits are determined by weighted sum of various commands that are scheduled on the memory interface.

The Intel I/O Controller Hub, ICH8, provides a bridge from the CPU to a variety of standardized interface with the target I/O device. Some of these I/O capabilities are:

- DMI interface provides high speed advanced priority-based servicing for concurrent traffic and true isochronous transfer capabilities.
- PCI Express interface provides 6 PCI Express root ports.
- Serial ATA (SATA) controller supports independent DMA operation on multiple ports and supports data transfer rates of up to 3.0 Gb/s.
- Advanced Host Controller Interface (AHCI) programming interface for SATA host controllers provides performance features such as each device treated as a master and hardware-assisted native command queuing.
- Intel Matrix Storage Technology provides both AHCI and integrated RAID functionality on SATA ports. Matrix RAID support provides the ability to combine multiple RAID levels on a single set of hard drives.
- Fast IDE interface provides an interface for IDE hard disks and ATAPI devices.
- Serial Peripheral Interface (SPI) provides an alternative interface for the BIOS flash device.
- Gigabit Ethernet Controller provides a system interface via a PCI function. The controller provides a full memory-mapped or I/O mapped interface and Direct Memory Addressing (DMA) mechanisms for high performance data transfers. Its bus master capabilities enable the component to process high-level commands and perform multiple operations. This lowers processor utilization by off-loading communication tasks from the processor.

- High definition audio controller provides a digital interface that can be used to attach different types of codecs, such as audio and modem codecs.
- Real-time clock (RTC) provides 256 bytes of battery-backed RAM that can keep track of the time of day and stores system data, even when the system is powered down.
- System Management Bus host interfaces provides the processor ability to initiate communications with SMBus peripherals (slaves) and also support slave functionality. It implements hardware-based Packet Error Checking for data robustness and the Address Resolution Protocol (ARP) to dynamically provide address to all SMBus devices.

- The platform also supports:
- Integrated graphics and memory controllers, built directly into the processor die, supporting lower power and smaller footprint for small form factor designs.
- Intel Streaming SIMD Extensions (SSE) 2 and Intel SSE3 enable software to accelerate data processing in specific areas, such as complex arithmetic and video decoding.
- Intel Hyper-Threading Technology, with two threads per core, that provides high performance-per watt efficiency in an in-order pipeline, and increased system responsiveness in multi-tasking environments. One execution core is seen as two logical processors, and parallel threads are executed on a single core with shared resources.
- Dynamic L2 cache sizing reduces leakage due to transistor sleep mode.

These platforms can handle data from multiple sources over high-bandwidth interconnects. These platforms can be used for creating solutions for print imaging, digital signage, interactive kiosks, point-of-sale terminals, thin clients, digital security systems, and residential gateways, surveillance, DVR, embedded boards, industrial control, and energy signage.

Thus, the single-core Intel Atom processors N450 offer robust performance and scalability for embedded systems in intelligent environments. The feature specifications are summarized in Table 3.3.

Table 3.3	Intel® Atom™ N450–based Intensive I/O Computing Platform
Processor	Intel® Atom™ N450 Processor
Process	45 nm
Clock speed	1.6 GHz
Platform TDP	7.9 W
Chipset	Intel® 82801HM I/O Controller
Platform technologies	Intel® 64 architecture Execute Disable Bit

Intel® Xeon® 5300–based High Performance Platform (Code Name Cranberry Lake)

Intel high performance embedded platforms consist of processors and chipsets focused on high compute performance, data integrity features, large memory footprint and high I/O throughput. These embedded platforms are used for embedded applications, communications and storage. They provide fast processing and virtualization.

Intelligent environments that can be built with such platforms include smart devices in storage area networks, network attached storage, routers, converged/unified communications platforms, sophisticated content firewalls, unified threat management systems, medical imaging, military signal and image processing, and telecommunications.

The Intel Xeon 5300–based high performance platform has the following characteristics:

- Processor is Intel Xeon Processor 5300
- MCH chipset is Intel 5100
- 65 nm process
- Single, dual or quad core
- Intel Core microarchitecture supports improved performance/watt
- Platform power savings from lower TDP in the MCH
- Efficient Intel I/O Controller Hub 9R
- Standard native DDR2 memory technology, with a maximum capacity of 48 GB
- Dual-processing capabilities provide up to eight high-performance cores per platform to run parallel tasks
- High levels of computing for threaded applications provide eight-thread, 64-bit and 32-bit processing capabilities
- The Intel Memory Controller Hub 5100 chipset has the following features:

- Supports quad-core Intel Xeon processor L 5318
- Supports I/O Controller Hub 9R
- FSB frequency: 1066 MHz
- Supported memory type/speed: DDR3 800/1066 RDIMM or UDIMM
- Maximum memory: 144 GB
- PCI Express 2x16
- 12 USB ports
- IDE/ATA support: 6 SATA
- TDP: 25.3 W

The feature specifications for the Intel® Xeon® 5300–based high performance platform are summarized in Table 3.4.

Table 3.4   Intel® Xeon® 5300–based High Performance Platform

Processor	Intel® Xeon® processor L5318
Process	65 nm
Clock speed	1.6 GHz
Platform TDP	70 W
Chipset	5100, ICH9R
Platform technologies	Enhanced Intel® SpeedStep® Technology (EIST) Intel® 64 architecture Intel Demand Based Switching (IDBS) Intel® Virtualization Technology (Intel® VT) for IA-32, Intel® 64 and Intel® Architecture (Intel® VT-x) Execute Disable Bit

Intel® Core™ 2 Duo–based High Density Platform (Code Name Eagle Heights)

These platforms provide high performance per watt. The feature specifications are summarized in Table 3.5.

Table 3.5   Intel® Core™ Duo–based High Density Platform

Processor	Intel® Core™ 2 Duo processor SU9300 / SL9380
Process	45 nm
Clock speed	1.2 GHz / 1.8 GHz
Platform TDP	22.4 W / 29.4 W
Chipset	3100
Platform technologies	Enhanced Intel® SpeedStep® Technology (EIST) Intel® 64 architecture Intel® Trusted Execution Technology (Intel TXT) Intel® Virtualization Technology (Intel® VT) for IA-32, Intel® 64 and Intel® Architecture (Intel® VT-x) Execute Disable Bit

Intel® EP80579 Integrated Processor (SoC)–based Small Form Factor Platform (Code Name Tolapai)

A system on a chip (SoC) is a single highly integrated chip with processor and multiple functional unites. Thus many embedded applications that require multiple chips can now work with a single chip. Thus the footprint in terms of thermal power is decreased and performance is increased. Many graphics accelerations and security functions can be performed in the chip hardware, thus improving the security and throughput of these complex functions. Their high speed I/O and communication interfaces and small form factor enables more embedded applications, especially in areas of security, communications, and industrial automation.

The Intel EP80579 Integrated Processor is Intel's first SoC. The Intel EP80579 Integrated Processor with Intel QuickAssist Technology architecture integrates on a single chip, processor and multiple functional units:

- Low power and high performance Intel architecture based CPU core
- Integrated Memory Controller Hub (IMCH)
- Integrated I/O Controller Hub (IICH)
- Security Services Unit (SSU) for security processing
- Acceleration Services Units (ASU) for high throughput packet processing

The Intel EP80579 Integrated Processor is based on Intel architecture. Intel QuickAssist Technology provides high performance packet processing and security capabilities. The Intel EP80579 Integrated Processor product line architecture has high processing performance, high performance/watt for small form factor designs and stringent power usage. It also has security accelerators for bulk encryption, hashing, and public/private key generation.

The Intel EP80579 Integrated Processor is a low-power and high-performance architecture based on an Intel architecture (IA-32) processor. The core is based on 90-nm process technology.

It operates on three operating frequencies up to 1.2 GHz. It has support for 32-bit physical addressing.

It has a 256 KB L2 data coherent cache, which is a two-way L2 unified pipelined non-blocking cache with 64-byte lines, and has soft-error protection on L2 cache data and tags (via parity).

The Integrated Memory Control Hub (IMCH) and Integrated I/O Control Hub (IICH) provide the following:

- Enhanced DMA (EDMA) controller performs background data transfers between locations in main memory, or from main memory to a memory-mapped I/O destination. These transfers may be individually designated to be coherent or non-coherent, providing improvements in system performance and utilization when cache coherence is managed by software rather than hardware.

- PCI Express interfaces support connection to other compatible PCI Express devices that may implement functionality such as graphics, hardware RAID controllers, and TCP/IP off-load engines. It supports hierarchical PCI-compliant configuration mechanism for downstream devices. It has a full-speed interface self-test and diagnostic (IBIST) functionality. It can do automatic discovery, negotiation, and training of PCI Express ports out of reset. It supports both coherent and non-coherent traffic to memory. Non-coherent implies a combination of Snoop-Not-Required and Relaxed-Ordering attributes. Coherent traffic implies a combination of Snoop-Required and Strong-Ordering attributes.

- Integrated Memory Controller Interface for direct-connection to a single channel of DDR2 (400, 533, 667, 800) or DDR3-800 unbuffered or registered memory devices. Peak theoretical memory data bandwidth using DDR2-800 or DDR3-800 is 6.4 gigabits per second. It supports optional error protection using ECC bits and error code that supports SEC/DED (single-bit error correction/double-bit error detection). On a single-bit error, the memory controller corrects the error bit and writes back the correct data value to DRAM, if enabled by software selection.

- SATA Gen1 or Gen2 interfaces
- USB 1.1 or USB 2.0 ports
- Integrated, 16550-compatible UARTs
- LPC 1.1 interface
- Serial Peripheral Interface (SPI)
- SMBus 2.0 interfaces
- GPIOs
- Watchdog timer
- 32/64-bit high-precision event timers

The Intel EP80579 Integrated Processor's Acceleration Services Unit (ASU) provides high performance acceleration hardware for network packet processing and on-chip security processing capability. ASU support capabilities for various protocol implementations such as TCP/IP, UDP, IPSec, and SSL.

The Intel EP80579 Integrated Processor's Security Services Unit (SSU) provides high-performance on-chip crypto accelerator and support capabilities for commonly used cryptographic protocol implementations.

Other features include:

- Gigabit Ethernet MACs providing 10/100/1000 ports with serial EEPROM interface supports network boot and wake-on LAN
- Integrated Serial ATA (SATA) Host Controllers provide independent DMA operation on two ports, data transfer rates up to 3.0 Gb/s, and alternate device ID
- Integrated high-speed serial interface (TDM)supports external T1/E1 and codecs and HDLC channels
- Dual Controller Area Network (CAN)interfaces
- Single Synchronous Serial Port (SSP)
- Gigabit Ethernet MAC (GbE) Control Area Network (CAN) interfaces
- 1088-Ball FCBGA package with Dimensions of 37.5 mm x 37.5 mm

The above features of the Intel EP80579 Integrated Processor make it a natural choice for embedded applications that require Intel architecture compatibility and high-speed interfaces like Gigabit Ethernet and PCI Express. It is also ideal for intelligent environments that run application security services and need packet security compatibility and IP Telephony packet security, TDM, and High-Level Data Link Control (HDLC).

The Intel EP80579 Integrated Processor gives footprint savings as compared to discrete multi-chip solutions. Integrated accelerators support Intel QuickAssist Technology via security and IP telephony software packages. These SoCs have great use in embedded systems, security, and communications. They can be used in a range of appliances for VPN and firewall, converged access platforms, IP media servers and VoIP gateways, network attached storage, converged IP PBX, and industrial automation applications. Table 3.6 summarizes the feature specifications.

Table 3.6   Intel® EP80579 Integrated Processor (SoC)–based Small Form Factor Platform

Processor	Intel® EP80579 Integrated Processor with Intel® Quick Assist Technology
Process	90 nm
Clock speed	0.6 GHz / 1.066 GHz / 1.2 GHz
Platform TDP	12 W / 20 W / 21 W
Platform technologies	Intel® Quick Assist Technology Execute Disable Bit

Mini SoC–based Platform (Code Name Tunnel Creek)

The processor code named Tunnel Creek is an Intel architecture CPU for the small form factor ultra low power embedded segments. It has a new architecture partitioning which integrates the 3D graphics engine, memory controller, video codec, display and other blocks with the Intel architecture CPU core.

Tunnel Creek is a "mini-SOC" that is complete in providing boot functionalities and Windows support.

It has an open-standard PCI Express v1.0 interface, which can enable any IOH, ASIC, FPGA and off-the-shelf discrete components. An example is a generic IOH through single x1 PCI-E connection. This flexibility in various kinds of I/O solutions is important for deeply embedded applications in intelligent environments, in which I/O differs from one application to another. For example, different IOH solutions can be built for the following applications:

- In-vehicle infotainment
- Residential gateway
- Media phone

Tunnel Creek has a low-power intel architecture core supporting frequency up to 1.3 GHz, with support for the following:

- On die 32 KB 4-way L1 instruction cache
- On die 24 KB 6-way L1 data cache
- On die 512 KB, 8-way L2 cache
- L2 dynamic cache sizing
- Intel Virtualization Technology
- Intel Hyper-Threading Technology
- Enhanced Intel SpeedStep Technology
- Intel Deep Power Down Technology (C6)
- Intel SSE2, Intel SSE3 and Supplemental SSE3

The Tunnel Creek System Memory Controller supports single-channel DDR2 memory with 32-bit data bus and a total memory size of up to 1 GB. It has aggressive power management to reduce power consumption, including shallow self-refresh and a new deep self-refresh support. It also proactively does page closing policies to close unused pages.

Tunnel Creek has an integrated 2D/3D graphic engine It has video decode support for MPEG2, MPEG4, VC1, WMV9, H.264, and DivX. It has video encode support for MPEG4, H.263, H.264, and VGA/QGA

Display interfaces support LVDS and Serial DVO (SDVO) display ports enabling simultaneous and independent operation of two displays. Low-Voltage Differential Signaling (LVDS) Interface enables the graphics and video adaptor to communicate directly to an on-board flat panel display. The LVDS interface supports a maximum resolution up to 1280 x 768 with 60Hz. It also has an LVDS backlight control related signal in order to support LVDS panel backlight adjustment. Serial DVO (SDVO) Display Interface is a digital display channel that can drive SDVO adapters that provide interfaces to a variety of external display technologies (such as DVI, TV-Out, and analog CRT). Maximum resolution is 1280 x 1024 at 85 Hz.

The PCIe ports may be used to attach discrete I/O components or a custom I/O Hub for increased I/O expansion. The four x1 PCIe ports operate as four independent PCIe controllers. Each root port supports up to 2.5 Gb/s bandwidth in each direction per lane.

An Intel High Definition Audio Controller provides a digital interface that can be used to attach different types of codecs (such as audio and modem codecs). The Intel HD Audio controller supports multi-channel audio stream, 32-bit sample depth, and sample rate up to 192 kHz. The Intel HD Audio controller uses a set of DMA engines to effectively manage the link bandwidth and support simultaneous independent streams on the link. The Intel HD Audio controller also supports isochronous data transfers allowing glitch-free audio to the system.

Other features are:

- SMBus Host Controller allows the processor to communicate with SMBus slaves. It can also initiate communications with SMBus peripherals (slaves)
- General Purpose I/O (GPIO), some of which are powered by core power rail and are turned off during sleep mode. Some others are powered by the suspend power well and remain active during sleep mode. Few can be used to wake the system from the Suspend-to-RAM state.
- The SPI interface provides access to the boot-flash, from which the system can be booted from.
- LPC is provides connectivity to a any IO chip, which may implement additional capabilities like UARTs and PS2 interfaces.
- Watchdog Timer (WDT), which is user configurable watchdog timer and contains selectable prescaler in range 1 μs–10 minutes
- Real Time Clock (RTC) provides a battery backed-up date and time keeping device. The time keeping comes from an oscillating source.

- Flip-Chip Ball Grid Array (FCBGA) package with dimensions 22 mm x 22 mm and Z-height of 2.097 mm–2.35 mm.

Tunnel Creek also allows flexible configuration of various device maintenance routines as well as power management functions including enhanced clock control and low-power state transitions. Software has the ability to work with low-power states thus enabling them to manage power efficiencies.

All these large number of computing, display and communication features in such a small, low power, many-in-one chip, makes it work so well in intelligent environments.

Intel® Xeon® 5500–based Bladed Form Factor Platform (Code Name Tylersburg High Tcase)

Intel Xeon processor–based platforms have lower thermal design power (TDP) and higher Tcase temperature systems. So they are suitable for intense computing embedded applications due to high performance and low power consumption.

The Intel Xeon processor 5500 series are based on the Intel microarchitecture code named Nehalem and implemented in 45 nm technology. They have thermal design power (TDP) less than 80 W. They have multiple cores and provide high performance and virtualization in bladed form factor.

Their high performance is due to:

- Integrated memory controller reduces memory latency.
- Automated low power states which put processor, memory and I/O controller into the lowest available power states possible with the current workload.
- Up to 144 GB of main memory provides high performance for data-intensive applications.
- Intel Virtualization Technology for Directed I/O gives designated virtual machines their own dedicated I/O devices
- Intel® QuickPath Technology, Intel Turbo Boost Technology and Intel Hyper-Threading Technology
- The Intel 5520 chipset provides up to 42 lanes of PCI Express, SATA ports, and support for RAID.

These platforms work well in thermally constrained applications and are compatible with enterprise platform configurations. All Intel Xeon processors based on the Intel microarchitecture code named Nehalem have a common electrical and mechanical socket providing a simplified path to future upgrades. The common microarchitecture and a common mechanical socket throughout both series provide investment protection and a simplified path to upgrades. The feature specifications are summarized in Table 3.7.

Table 3.7   Intel® Xeon® 5500-based Bladed Form Factor Platform (code named Tylersburg High Tcase)

Processor	Intel® Xeon® processor L5508 / L5518
Process	45 nm
Clock speed	2.0 GHz / 2.13 GHz
Platform TDP	69.6 W / 91.6 W
Chipset	5520, ICH10R
Platform technologies	Enhanced Intel® SpeedStep® Technology (EIST) Intel® 64 architecture delivers 64-bit computing and allows systems to address more than 4 GB of both virtual and physical memory. Intel® Hyper-Threading Technology (Intel HT Technology) Intel® Virtualization Technology (Intel VT) Execute Disable Bit

Intel® Core™ i5-based Scalable Platform (Code Name Fox Hollow)

Intel's scalable platforms can handle data from multiple sources over high-bandwidth interconnects. They also give performance and power efficiency with graphics, memory, and I/O to handle a broad range of application requirements.

Fox Hollow combines the Intel Core i5 processor and Intel 3450 chipset on same platform. Due to its Intel Core microarchitecture on 32 nm process technology and the Intel 3450 chipset, this platform provides advanced technologies like graphics, security, and remote manageability for embedded applications. The feature specifications are summarized in Table 3.8.

The Intel 3450 chipset on the platform provides error correcting code (ECC) memory, and the ability to correct memory errors without requiring system reset. This capability is of importance for system uptime and autonomous operation required in remote embedded systems.

Other features of this platform are:

- The Intel Core i5-660 supports Intel® vPro™ technology, which provides hardware support to enable security and system management functions.
- Flexible x16 PCI Express 2.0 controller integrated in the processor
- 2 channel DDR3 memory up to 16 GB
- PCH provides additional USB, PCI Express, and SATA ports

- PCH supports two display streams that can be used with HDMI, DVI, SDVO, or VGA
- High definition audio
- Gigabit Ethernet controller

Table 3.8   Intel® Core™ i5-based Scalable Platform

Processor	Intel® Core™ i5-660 Processor
Process	32 nm
Clock Speed	3.33 GHz
Platform TDP	77.7 W
Chipset	3450
Platform Technology	Enhanced Intel® SpeedStep® Technology (EIST) Intel® 64 architecture Intel® Active Management Technology (Intel AMT6) Intel® Hyper-Threading Technology (Intel HT Technology) Intel® Trusted Execution Technology (Intel TXT) Intel® Virtualization Technology (Intel VT) Execute Disable Bit

Thus, these platforms can be used for developing high-performance systems for different applications in intelligent environments, namely, industrial control and automation, retail, gaming, print imaging and digital signage.

Intel's IVI Open Infotainment Platform with FPGA (OIP)

Intelligent vehicles have wirelessly connected in-vehicle infotainment (IVI) systems that keep travelers linked to homes and offices even as they are in their cars.

Intel enables technologies to support people in their home and office multi-media based experiences. The vehicles become a natural extension of that when they are on road. The on-road digital lifestyle includes autonomous navigation, rear-seat entertainment, telematics capabilities, and devices such as MP3 players and phones. The vehicles can even find the nearest electrical recharge station, and help smooth out traffic jams.

Intel Atom processor–based Open Infotainment Platforms enable integration of the in-vehicle infotainment capabilities and utilizes same common hardware and software architecture, the OS, middleware, and the application level. All applications for both driver and rear-seat passengers can be integrated into the same system.

The Intel Atom processor uses the same consistent instruction set as other Intel processors to create new products. Nearly any software written for PCs and mobile Internet devices can run on the Intel Atom processor. Intel

Atom processor is based on the same x86 instruction set used by chips in PCs for almost three decades. This also gives the flexibility for many onboard automotive custom-built applications for 8- or 16-bit microprocessors that control very specific tasks, such as antilock braking, airbag deployment, or body control.

The Low-Power Intel® In-Vehicle Infotainment Reference Design based OIP addresses requirements for in-car operating conditions, as well as quality and reliability standards. The integrated platform incorporates a variety of IVI features to simplify development.

A small footprint, efficient thermal design and compact I/O interfaces fit into a standard, single DIN slot, making it ideal for IVI applications. Low-power characteristics of the platform, based on the Intel® Atom™ processor Z530Δ, Intel® System Controller Hub US15W and fanless thermal solution, help eliminate noise and reliability concerns related to the use of fans and heat sinks.

A low-power Intel In-Vehicle Infotainment system based on Intel Atom (used for POS, medical, healthcare, kiosk, gaming, digital signage) could have the following features:

- Intel® Embedded Compact Extended Form Factor
- Compact size with fan-less design
- Intel® ECX Form Factor single board computer
- 6V ~ 24V wide DC power input
- DVB-T/FM tuner, Wi-Fi† and 3 SDIO sockets integrated
- Dual-display support (VGA and LVDS)
- Standard multimedia functions for audio and video
- TPM (Trusted Platform Module)
- UDM (USB-Disk Module)
- Open architecture for easy customization
- System Specifications:
- CPU: Intel® Atom™ processor Z510
- Chipset: Intel® System Controller Hub US15W
- System memory: one 200-pin SO-DIMM supports DDR2-533 SDRAM up to 1 GB
- Display: Intel® GMA 500
- Expansion: one MiniCard (PCI-Express x1 + USB interface)
- Peripherals: TV/FM tuner, Bluetooth†, Wi-Fi, and GPS modules
- Storage: one 2.5" HDD and one CompactFlash socket
- Front panel specifications

- LED indicators: HDD, Suspend mode, power
- Power: one power ON/OFF button
- SDIO: SDIO slot
- Two USB ports
- Rear I/O specifications
- Display: VGA
- Audio: CH5.1 audio
- COM: one RS-232 serial port
- USB: four USB ports
- Power: 6V~24V DC-IN
- Antenna: Antenna connection for Wi-Fi or TV tuner

This open platform is characterized by:

- Intel Atom Processor Z530 at 1.6 GHz and Intel System Controller Hub US15W, which meet developer requirements for high-performance, highly integrated, low-power solutions
- Easy integration of PC-based applications
- Thermally efficient embedded designs
- Full-featured embedded operating systems
- Wireless networking options, including 3G cellular and Wi-Fi
- Intel Hyper-Threading Technology (Intel HT Technology)
- Intel Virtualization Technology (Intel VT)
- The industrial temperature option of the Intel Atom processor Z5xx platform, validated for the -40°+85° C temperature range
- Infotainment features such as 3D navigation, rear-seat entertainment, cameras and Internet connectivity
- Dual independent display for display terminals in both front and rear seats
- Dual independent audio stream for both front and rear seats
- Consolidated I/O connector supports ease of integration
- AM/FM tuner
- Daughter card system allows designers flexibility to design custom cards based on individual needs.
- Low-power system controller daughter card module supports power management, wakeup, and startup/shutdown control.
- Designed for rapid access to video from cameras connected to the infotainment system

- Intel® architecture technology is fully interoperable with existing home and office technology
- Wide battery operation range (8-20V), protection and multiple wakeup options including ignition allow for quick integration into a vehicle environment

Automotive FPGA

The Low-Power Intel IVI Reference Design can use an FPGA to extend the platform's flexibility and integrate many automotive-specific functions such as video and MOST network connectivity. Using the FPGA, designers are able to build upon an available platform to produce a customized peripheral extension chip to the Intel System Controller Hub US15W. A standard adaption guide allows the user to add or remove peripherals in the FPGA and to scale the device density for the optimal solution. The standard design incorporates multiple functions including:

- Additional I2C, I2S, and UART connectivity
- Video frame grabber input for camera connectivity
- SDHC v2.0 for high-capacity storage
- MOST connectivity through FPGA

FPGA can be used instead of mask programmed ASICs and ASSPs. FPGAs avoid the high initial mask set costs and lengthy development cycles. They allow design upgrades without hard-ware replacement.

Support for typical in-vehicle infotainment connectivity functions includes:

- Bluetooth wireless connectivity to cell phones for hands-free use
- Video capture for side- and rear-view cameras
- Stereo line-in and line-out, and microphone through connectors
- Four external and two internal USB connectors for GPS, MP3 players, DVD players, and other consumer electronic devices
- PCI Express port for I/O peripheral expansion and flexible connectivity
- SDIO V2.0 support of SDHC for high-capacity storage
- CAN network connectivity and wakeup on CAN activity functionality
- SDVO-to-LVDS video encoder for plug-in connectivity to additional displays
- PATA connector for hard disk drives
- Ethernet to download software updates and simplify diagnostics
- FPGA for additional custom logic

- Feature characteristics:
- Processor Intel® Atom™ processor Z530
- Chipset Intel® System Controller Hub US15W
- Dimensions 165-mm wide by 175-mm deep supports standard DIN slot
- Peripheral extension FPGA chip
- Operating system drivers for a variety of operating systems
- Memory 1 GB DDR2 533 MHz
- Hard disk interface: one PATA connector supporting up to two drives
- Display interface: primary: LVDS; secondary: LVDS or VGA
- Audio interface through connector: line-in L/R, line-out L/R, SPDIF 5.1, stereo microphone
- I/O connectivity: six USB ports, one serial port, one Ethernet RJ-45 connector
- Expansion card options Wi-Fi, TV tuner
- Power supply Wide range (8-20V)

Power and Thermal Management in Intel Platforms:

There are temperature gradients on the die. Digital thermal sensing is used to provide temperature readings. This enables higher CPU performance within thermal limitations and improves reliability.

Hardware Thermal Status Exposure

Thermal and power management can be balanced. DTS and PECI help software control the balance through hardware thermal monitoring and control.

Recent Intel architecture processors including Intel Xeon processors in platforms like the Intel Embedded Performance DP Bladed Platform for 2008 (code named Cranberry Lake) support thermal monitoring in three ways:

- TM1 (Thermal Monitor 1) and TM2 (Thermal Monitor 2)
- DTS (Digital Thermal Sensors) for each core
- PECI (Platform Environment Control Interface) access to processor thermal data

DTS enables processor thermal control. Several thermal sensors are located within the Processor to cover all possible hot spots. Dedicated logic scans the thermal sensors and measures the maximum temperature on the die at any given time. It then accurately reports processor temperature. This enables advanced thermal control schemes by the software. The Intel Xeon 5500 processor contains a Digital Thermal Sensor (DTS) that reports a relative die temperature as an offset from Thermal Control Circuit (TCC) activation temperature. Temperature sensors located throughout the die are implemented as analog-to-digital converters calibrated at the factory. The data reported in DTS reflects the delta between the current temperature and the maximum junction temperature of the die.

The Platform Environmental Control Interface (PECI) is an Intel proprietary interface that provides a communication channel between Intel processors and chipset components to external thermal monitoring devices. Using PECI, processor provides its temperature reading over a multi drop single wire bus allowing efficient platform thermal control. PECI is the bridge between applications and hardware to read DTS data and other information. Software can take advantage of PECI to monitor the processor temperature. PECI provides an interface for external devices to read the processor temperature, perform processor manageability functions, and manage processor interface tuning and diagnostics:

-
- PECI is used for monitoring thermals on processors
- Single wire interface used to access processor temperature data
- Multi-drop bus scales with dual processors and multi-core processors
- PECI pollers periodically query each processor for temperature data
- Processor reports digital thermal sensor (DTS) offset from Thermal Control Circuit (TCC) activation temperature.
- Can also be used to control fan speed

DTS and PECI are mechanisms that allow software to monitor processor temperature. The DTS can be used to monitor silicon junction temperature. PECI is used to focus on the hottest DTS value.

The thermal data can be obtained by Model Specific Register (MSR) access or Platform Environment Control Interface (PECI) and used by the system for fan speed control or used by customers to develop advanced power management and thermal control schemes.

Thermal control mechanisms are controlled by the same DTS values that are read over PECI bus (through an MSR) so these temperature values give warning for thermal events like throttling. Thermal control is achieved by adjusting the fan speed through the PECI.

Hardware Thermal Control Signals

Most Intel processors implement hardware-based thermal control. Hardware-based thermal management handles abnormal thermal conditions and protects the die from transient effects. Hardware-based thermal control ensures that the CPU will never cross specified conditions. This allows higher performance with tighter control parameters.

Intel architecture processors provide the capability of shutdown when processor core temperature rises above a factory-set limit.

Thermal control features implement two externally visible signals:

- THERMTRIP: a fixed temperature sensor to detect catastrophic thermal conditions and to shut down the system if thermal runaway occurs.
- THERMTRIP# will be asserted to indicate the processor junction temperature has reached a point beyond which permanent silicon damage may occur.
- The response to THERMTRIP# is that the processor will shut off its internal clocks to reduce the processor junction temperature.
- Then core voltage VCC will be removed. THERMTRIP# remains asserted only until PWRGOOD is de-asserted.
- Initiated by processor temperature
- Processor shuts down if THERMTRIP temperature set point reached
- Benefits are it protects processor from damage during catastrophic cooling failure
- PROCHOT: a fixed temperature threshold that provides a self-control mechanism that drops frequency and voltage to a new working point

- Thermal control signals in Cranberry Lake:
- PROCHOT (Processor Hot)
- Output signal
- Asserted at pre-set trip point, at or a few degrees above maximum TCASE when dissipating TDP power
- FORCEPR
- Asynchronous Input Signal
- Asserted by external source such as overheating power supply to activate the Thermal Control Circuit (TCC) for both processor cores.
- TCC remains active until the system deasserts FORCEPR
- THERMTRIP
- Output Signal

- Triggers catastrophic shutdown when THERMTRIP temperature is reached
- Enabled after PWRGOOD and disabled on deassertion of PWRGOOD
- If junction temperature is above trip level, THERMTRIP will reassert after PWRGOOD assertion

Thermal Monitoring Mechanisms

Two automatic thermal monitoring mechanisms (TM1 and TM2) can force the processor to reduce its power consumption.

- TM1 controls the processor core temperature by modulating the duty cycle of processor clock. TM1 trips when the core temperature crosses a certain level.
- TM2 controls processor core temperature by reducing the operating frequency and voltage of the processor.

The thermal monitors remain engaged until the processor core temperature drops below the preset trip temperature of the temperature sensor. While the processor is in a stop-clock state, interrupts will be blocked from interrupting the processor. This holding off of interrupts increases the interrupt latency, but does not cause interrupts to be lost. Outstanding interrupts remain pending until clock modulation is complete.

Both thermal monitors TM1 and TM2 are initiated by processor temperature. TM1 modulates processor clock on/off to reduce processor temperature. TM2 reduces processor frequency and voltage to reduce processor temperature. Benefits are it maintains system operation uptime during high temperature transients

Thermal control directly translates to power control. The two can be balanced. Software can use thermal headroom to increase application performance. When applications are sensitive about power consumption, they can use processor thermal data to reduce consumption.

Thermal monitoring features in Cranberry Lake:

- Thermal monitor (TM1)
- Helps control the processor temperature by activating Thermal Control Circuit (TCC) when the processor silicon reaches its maximum operating temperature.
- When activated, the clocks will be modulated by alternately turning the clocks off and on at a duty cycle specific to the processor
- Cycle times are processor speed dependent and will decrease as processor core frequencies increase.

- Enhanced Thermal Monitor (TM2)
- The TCC causes the processor to adjust its operating frequency and input voltage.
- This combination of reduced frequency and Voltage results in a reduction to the processor power consumption
- Two operating points (normal operating point and lower operating points) are specified each consisting of a specific operating frequency and voltage
- When activated, transitions to lower frequency rapidly
- All bus traffic blocked during transition

Conclusion

Intel architecture combines building blocks like processors and SoCs to create platforms. Platforms are a validated combination of an Intel processor and Intel chipset. Intel's newest platforms offer robustness, scalability, low power, and high performance in a small form factor.

We have seen how different Intel embedded building blocks can be put together to create different platforms that have for small form factor, high performance, low power needs, and are scalable. Now we discuss various ways in which Intel technologies and other industry innovations can be used to create solutions for intelligent environments like intelligent retail, intelligent energy grids, and intelligent signage.

4

Intelligent Environments for Energy

I ntelligent environments are everywhere in the sphere of energy. The transition to renewable sources of energy requires the energy environments to be even more intelligent.

Introduction

The energy value chain can be divided into three main activities, all of which can carry embedded intelligence:
- Smart energy generation
- Smart energy transmission and distribution
- Smart energy consumption

Intelligence in Energy: Smart Generation, Smart Distribution, Smart Consumption

Embedded intelligence enables every component of the intelligent energy environments:
- Smart generation: wind turbines and solar stations that generate energy
- Smart distribution: smart grids control systems that distribute power
- Smart consumption: smart meters that monitor home consumption, smart infrastructure, like smart street lights, smart commercial energy management systems

If the generation system is on grid, distribution and transmission take place over large distances and complex networks, and different grids are connected to arbitrage power surplus and deficit across an entire network. Off-grid systems, on the other hand, typically have little transmission and distribution, except, for example, local generation for gated communities or small villages.

Apart from thermal power, there are renewable energy generation systems. These include hydroelectric, geothermal, tidal, wind, solar, photovoltaic, thermal, and biomass-based gasifiers. The gasifiers can be direct-fired boilers and biomass-to-liquid-to-power technologies. Most of these systems are variable-output, often linked to large energy storage units, and require a high degree of intelligent intervention to optimize performance.

On the consumption side, carbon footprint mitigation is done through smart lighting, intelligent space heating/cooling/dehumidification, auto-shut-off devices for high-load appliances such as water heaters and air conditioners.

Intel processors, chipsets, and advanced technologies can bring end-to-end intelligence to a smart grid at all its various components, namely: smart energy generation, smart energy distribution, and smart energy consumption.

Intel® architecture and Intel hardware's compute and communications capabilities can enable smart power routing, management, control, and metering functions between the consumer end points and generating stations.

A smart grid delivers electricity from generators to consumers using two-way power flow as well as two way digital communications. It combines the electricity distribution grid, digital control, and net metering system. This enables routing energy in more optimal ways in a sustainable manner.

A smart grid is interactive with two-way real-time communication, multi-directional energy flow, and closed-loop automation.

- Smart energy generation enables the integration and optimization of more renewable energy like solar and wind
- Smart energy distribution increases efficiencies of our energy network and provide real-time knowledge and control over the distribution in smart grids.
- Smart energy consumption enables consumers to manage their energy usage by providing real-time knowledge and decision-making tools

Smart energy generation from renewable energy resources, like wind and solar, are variable in energy output.

Intel technologies can help with forecasts, analysis, prediction, and integrate them into the first tier sustainable energy sources. Energy generation by multiple alternative sources means power enters the network from multiple locations in the distributed generation network.

Smart energy distribution can be enabled by Intel architecture to provide distributed management and control of the smart grid. Intelligence in energy distribution enables monitoring, self-healing, and automation, helping prevent trouble before it occurs. Monitoring and diagnostics reduce unexpected transformer failure and subsequent power outages. By smart sensor monitoring, problems are detected in real time or even before time.

Smart energy consumption enables demand response and home energy management can be done using Intel architecture–based management and control inside the home. Such demand response and dynamic demand mechanisms based on feedback mechanisms manage customer consumption of electricity in response to supply conditions, such as, for example, having electricity customers reduce their consumption at critical times or in response to market prices. Smart energy consumption utilizes various technologies in the home like smart meters, smart energy panels, and smart appliances. Smart meters as well as smart metering infrastructure help reduce consumption smartly. Some examples of possible intelligence in smart grids:

- Smart energy generation:
    - o Embedded Intel rugged platforms in wind turbines:
    - o Enable guide vanes to tell the direction of the wind
    - o Control the guide vane's pitch, rotation, and functions
    - o Enable guide vanes response in real time to changing wind conditions
- Smart energy distribution:
    - o Computing based on Intel processors for substation control:
    - o Control operations of electrical transmission and distribution network
    - o Manage the flow and distribution of energy within the network
    - o Consolidate relays, remote terminal units, and data aggregation
- Smart energy consumption:
    - o Smart in-home displays based on Intel processors
    - o Enable profile, monitor, and manage domestic energy usage
    - o Enable customers benefit from demand-response programs
    - o Home energy management systems based on Intel processors
    - o Enable energy efficiency programs, and demand-response signals
    - o Enable energy savings both for consumers and utilities

Intel advanced technologies can be used for remote monitoring; virtualization and security help mitigate the problem in real time before sending a repair crew.

There is a paradigm shift from centralized control of the energy network to a model of distributed control and intelligence, which is needed to use distributed energy generation sources such as wind and solar. Thus intelligence is deployed at every node throughout the network to achieve end-to-end energy flow management, control and feedback through the smart grids. Intelligence in smart grids, along with smart devices, automation technologies, and applications that adapt in real time, help utilities improve power reliability.

Smart Distribution of Energy

Smart energy distribution systems have distributed computing intelligence. Intelligence is distributed such that decision making is localized near the sources of information as well as the point of control. Smart energy distribution also has intelligence to aggregate information from various local systems, such as smart meters and substations. Then it uses this context awareness to smartly control the grid system. Both kinds of embedded intelligence can be enabled by Intel technologies.

Intel's embedded building blocks can enable more intelligence within the grid, wind turbines that generate energy, control systems that distribute power, and smart meters that manage consumption.

Smart distribution of energy has the following goals:

- Optimize energy capacity
- Utilize renewable energy sources
- Manage demand
- Ensure availability
- Improved reliability
- Stronger security

Smart Energy Grids with Intelligence

Smart grids deliver electricity from generators to consumers, in an intelligent manner, using digital technologies to modernize the distribution of energy. Smart grids have the following intelligent characteristics:

- Monitor real time energy flow and take control action (optimize efficiency)
- Receive energy from generators like photovoltaic, wind (optimize generation)
- Provide energy to consumers in homes and other places (optimize consumption)
- Integrate consumers who at times generate energy (bidirectional metering)
- Integrate new paradigms like plug-in hybrid vehicles (point of sale metering)

Intel technologies can enable intelligence in all of these characteristics.

- Intelligence of smart grids consists of intelligent components like soft PLCs and relay controllers that ensure availability, predictability, and efficiencies.
- Intel processors, chipsets, and advanced technologies can provide the following capabilities needed for reliability in energy management:
- Remote management: remote diagnostic and repair capabilities can make equipment more available
- Virtualization: isolating application code and preventing dangerous interactions can make software reliable
- Security: preventing any node from executing malicious software can provide grid security

The smart grid combines power transmission and information technologies, creating a bidirectional flow of energy and programs that can optimize energy usage.

Such smart grids are characterized by:

- Power flow in both directions since generation is distributed
- Programs are distributed thus data/information flows both ways
- Computing ability
- Security ability
- Networking ability

Intel silicon components can bring:

- Remote management, with Intel® Advanced Management Technology (Intel AMT) on hardware.
- Virtualization, with Intel® Virtualization Technology (Intel VT) on hardware
- Security, with Intel® Trusted Execution Technology (Intel TXT) on hardware
- Performance headroom with multiple cores technology supply the computing power required in smart grids
- Lower power consumption when processing workload decreases.

Some examples of intelligence in smart energy grid management include:

- Computing power
- High-performance processors with multi-core technology
- Fanless systems with small form factor requirements.

- Remote diagnostic and repair capabilities
- Software reliability by isolating application code
- Grid security by preventing any node from executing malicious software

Remote Management with Intel® AMT for Systems Online Availability

Intel AMT–based remote management technologies can help diagnose, repair, and get equipment back online for smart grids.

Intel Active Management Technology (Intel AMT) implements a special circuit in the Intel chipset that can access and control the system, even when the system is powered off or the software is corrupted.

This circuit establishes an "out-of-band" link that allows the system to communicate with a management console with-out relying on the system's standard networking functionality. Intel AMT can enable:

- Restoring hung systems by cycling power or booting over the network.
- Tracking intermittent failures by accessing error log from the remote console
- Protecting against infected devices by quarantine at-risk systems
- Fixing remotely system defects and track inventory
- Changing remotely BIOS configuration settings even system not running.
- Keeping system virus signatures up-to-date without user assistance

Virtualization with Intel® VT Reliability for Control System Software Reliability

Safety-critical code should be run in safe, virtualized execution environments that isolate different workloads and prevent them from interfering with one another. Intel Virtualization Technology (Intel VT) can provide control over operating systems and applications.

This capability can simplify the porting of legacy applications onto new platforms, increase the performance of time-critical functions and avoid hardware rebooting delays.

Applications requiring a higher level of security should be isolated in secure virtual machines (VMs), whose memory space is protected. This can be enabled by hardware features in Intel processors and Intel VT. This means software running in a VM only has access to its own code and data regions, unable to page outside the memory boundaries specified by the Virtual Machine Manager (VMM)

Virtualization can be used to restart the software running in one partition without impacting the other partitions. This feature can be used for software failover mechanisms.

Software can be safeguarded using virtualization with Intel VT:

- Isolate applications in secure partitions
- Software migration and consolidation
- Run RTOS on a dedicated processor core
- Real-time performance
- Restart applications without booting the hardware
- System starts working

Protecting Against Software-based Attacks with Intel® TXT

Intel Trusted Execution Technology (Intel TXT) can integrate security capabilities into the processor, chipset, and other platform components. These hardware-based security features can be used to run applications in a safe partition and thus protect crucial platform data.

Malicious software can be stopped from executing by using hardware-based security features. This technology can create a trusted execution environment, such that only applications or device drivers on a trusted list can be loaded.

Intel TXT software can protect data from hackers by running applications, operating systems and VMMs in the highest privilege level, permission granted only by system developers.

Intel TXT can prevent spoofing and phishing attacks by providing sealed storage in the TPM for security codes, like VPN encryption keys.

Intel TXT can encrypt and stores critical security codes and ensures they are only decrypted in the executing environment that originally encrypted them.

Intel TXT can stop compromised systems from booting whenever the software or hardware configuration differs from the trusted state. Intel TXT compares the hash with the current state and blocks system startup when differences are detected.

Protect against software-based attacks using Intel TXT by:

- Protecting execution environment
- Safeguarding critical applications and data like encrypted keys and secrets
- Eliminating potential security holes
- Preventing compromised systems from booting
- Restricted launch environment
- Preventing execution of untrusted software

Intel product technologies can provide capabilities for simplifying software consolidation, managing equipment remotely, and increasing system security.

Smart Generation of Energy

Smart generation of energy entails local intelligence on turbines to do data preprocessing before sending data over LAN, the ability to evaluate and respond to weather conditions, and employing computationally intensive systems in the network for predicting energy demand, factoring in weather conditions, and minimizing the running out or storage of energy.

Smart generators like smart wind turbines can evaluate changing weather conditions like wind direction and respond by adjusting the position of turbine blades in real-time.

In wind turbines, intelligent control of the guide vane's pitch, rotation, and functions and rugged embedded Intel architecture platforms allow guide vanes to respond to changing wind conditions in real time.

Controllers based on energy-efficient Intel processors are sealed, fanless, and can withstand demanding environmental conditions.

Smart Wind Turbines with Intel Technologies

The power of the smart grid is in its ability to reallocate resources and thus its ability to move energy from places where the wind is blowing to where it is not.

The major requirement of smart grids utilizing wind turbines is reliability and availability of all components of the smart grid infrastructure, consisting of:

- Systems generating energy (smart generation)
- Systems controlling distribution (smart distribution)
- Systems consuming energy (smart consumption)

Wind turbines extract energy from winds. A wind turbine is like a giant fan spinning in reverse and generating energy with its mechanical motion.

The wind strikes its blades. The blades start rotating. That rotation drives a shaft connected to a generator. The generator produces electrical energy. This energy is sent on to power substations.

Intelligence in Smart Turbines

Uninterrupted operation of remote offshore wind turbines and other systems generating energy can be ensured by using Intel hardware and advanced technologies for remote management and virtualization.

Each turbine-mounted controller can be based on Intel low voltage processors, which can support 10/100Base-T Fast Ethernet ports, and DC power sources.

The energy efficiency of the embedded Intel architecture components enables controllers with sealed fanless construction to withstand demanding environmental conditions, and anti-vibration capabilities to ensure maximum mean time before failure (MTBF). Intel architecture enables easy integration and maintenance. Embedded Intel architecture components in wind turbine-mounted controllers would have the following characteristics:

• Ultra low voltage Intel processors
• 10/100Base-T Fast Ethernet ports
• DC power sources
• Energy efficiency
• Sealed fanless construction
• Anti-vibration capabilities
• Ability to withstand extreme environments
• Localized intelligence
• Embedded wind turbine controllers
• Rugged embedded Intel architecture platforms
• Real time response without human intervention
• Ability to control turbine vane pitch, rotation, and so on in response to changing wind conditions and electrical load requirements
• Local sensing
• Network sensors mounted on the turbine to communicate data to the embedded computer to monitor operating parameters including bearing temperature and vibration
• Remote monitoring
• Diagnostic data for each turbine easily monitored in real time by technicians in a control centers

Intel Remote Management in Smart Wind Turbines with Intel® AMT

Intel Active Management Technology (Intel AMT) can be used by the operations team to access and control a smart wind turbine controller even when the system software is corrupted. It implements a special circuit in the Intel chipset that can access and service the turbine controller, whether or not key hardware and software components are functional.

This circuit establishes an out-of-band link that allows the system to communicate with a management console without relying on the system's standard networking functionality. Even if the unit is powered off, diagnostics and many repairs can be accomplished remotely.

Intel AMT can support the wind farm infrastructure, wind turbines, control stations, and power substations. Thus Intel Active Management Technology can enable uninterrupted wind turbine availability.

Intel® Virtualization Technology (Intel VT) in Smart Wind Turbines

Intel VT can do various virtualization tasks in hardware, like memory address translation, to reduce the footprint of virtualization software and improve its performance. Intel VT can restore systems by cycling power, reloading software, or booting from hard drives over the network.

Intel VT can be used to track wind turbine components. It enables identifying installed hardware and software components, even if the turbine is not running, thus making it easier to diagnose and repair any faults.

Intel VT can be used to monitor intermittent failures and access system error logs and event records from flash at all times to the remote console.

Intel VT can isolate applications in secure partitions. This prevents software applications from interfering with one another. This also provides a software failover mechanism. Isolated virtualized environments isolate different workloads and prevent them from interfering with one another.

Intel VT can run an RTOS on a dedicated processor core. This improves real-time determinism. This also eases software consolidation.

Intel VT can help restart applications without booting the hardware. This gets the system working fast. This also resolves potentially catastrophic failure condition. Virtualization can be used to restart failing software running in one partition without impacting the software executing in other partitions.

Intel VT can be used to recover systems after software failure. This is done by quickly failover to a clean software copy using virtualization.

Intel VT enables real-time functions, like controlling the position of the rotor that cannot afford to share interrupts or CPU resources. Any possible contention is eliminated with virtualization and multi-core processors. Time-critical functions can be run on a real-time OS and on a dedicated processor core.

Remote management, virtualization and wireless technologies in both turbine and wind farm infrastructure make the smart wind turbines highly available.

Smart Consumption of Energy

Smart consumption of energy manages demand at the consumer end. To optimize use of energy, utility companies have time-of-day usage fees and dynamic pricing.

Keeping track of and controlling energy consumption can be done with help of intelligence in smart streetlights and smart energy management systems.

Intelligence in Smart Street Lights

Smart street lights are an adaptive, automated, and monitored lighting infrastructure system.

This system consumes minimal energy, ensures working infrastructure, and provides maximum lighting needed. This control is exerted at every single light bulb in the infrastructure.

Intelligent street lights dynamically adapt their own street light performance according to the actual needs for the given situation/period/time. Examples include:

- Environments such hospitals
- Situations such as an emergency or accident
- Weather such as wet or dry ground
- Usage such as traffic density
- Safety such as in a complex street

Smart street lights can also lower light output under good driving conditions, low traffic volumes, and low average speed.

The key goals of intelligent street lights are:

- Low energy consumption
- High functionality
- Low maintenance costs
- High safety

Intelligence in Street Lights takes the following forms:

- Environmental sensing

- Can sense environment by sensors for temperature, moisture, visibility, light intensity, rain and traffic density
- Wireless communication
- Can send sensed environmental data for remote analysis
- Remote assessment
- Can remotely assess condition and the light controlled remotely
- Can optimize lifespan of lights
- Can do maintenance scheduling efficiently
- Remote Control:
- Streetlights update the database periodically with sensor readings
- Servers can automatically control lights by sending network messages
- Monitoring the failure rate of each light in the streetlight network
- Can predict failures before they occur
- Web access: can monitor streetlight networks from any PC over the Internet

Components of Intelligent Street Light based on Intel Atom

Intelligent street lights can be enabled by Intel technologies:

The Intel embedded processors like the Intel Atom in industrial temperature versions have a small form factor and can be used for thermally constrained and fanless computers in extremes of temperature, dust, and humidity.

Intelligent street lighting infrastructure also includes wireless sensors, dimmable lights, advanced lighting control systems, and communication systems.

The major components are:

- Embedded wireless microcontrollers for streetlight control
- Networking that can self heal around any nodes that go faulty. It can automatically reform itself after any power disruptions.
- Network Control Center: servers to maintain the database of streetlights.
- Wireless communications: streetlights can communicate with data center using technologies such as GPRS, GSM, and Ethernet.
- Gateways: street light controllers communicates with the data center through gateways.
- Wirelessly connected sensors, one on each light pole, are connected through a self-configuring mesh network to access gateway devices enabled by energy-efficient Intel embedded processors.

- Each gateway device can support hundreds of sensors, and then securely transmit real-time data to a protected server.
- Each access point can be programmed to adjust light output to traffic or weather conditions to save electricity.
- Wireless gateways to support cellular network connectivity enables direct control of street lights by authorized personnel using a cell phone.

- Capabilities of intelligent street lights include:
- Adaptive lighting
- Performance monitoring of individual lights
- Measuring and analyzing power consumption
- Turning on flashing street lights in emergency situations
- Controlling programmable electronic signage mounted on light poles
- Not controlled by photocells that turn on/off at night/dusk
- Lights burn at an adaptive rate at needed power level throughout the night
- Nonworking street lights, lights, or photocells are automatically detected and alert messages sent for repairs
- Flexible control over lighting levels at each pole to match actual local requirements, such as automobile and pedestrian traffic volume, ambient light levels and weather conditions
- Monitoring of individual street lights to anticipate light and photocell failures before they occur
- Direct control of street lights by authorized personnel using a cell phone.

- Some examples of intelligence in smart street lights include:
- Illumination at maximum intensity during an emergency
- Illumination at maximum intensity within areas of road maintenance
- On-demand illumination triggered by traffic motion sensors
- Automatic illumination control based on traffic density sensors
- Illumination by pedestrians using roadway push button or cell phone text
- Automatically adjustable level of illumination based on the local weather
- Data collected from traffic sensors sent to the traffic management system
- Data collected from temperature sensors sent to maintenance operations
- Automatic pole damage detection and repair
- Automatic control of traffic speed by dimming of the streetlights
- Intelligent control increases light life

Thus, intelligent street lights can provide real-time data cities and power utilities to help reduce electric power consumption and maintenance costs.

Intelligence in Smart Commercial Energy Monitoring

Commercial energy monitoring needs fine-grained energy consumption monitoring, management, and control in buildings. Smart utility metering requires any sub-premise level or circuit level visibility, warnings on very costly usage of utilities or infrastructure, analytics like reduction goals, and so on. Intelligence in building management systems should have considerations for energy focus like energy load. Thus smart commercial energy monitoring systems need multi-sensor capable, real-time visibility and analysis ability. They also need to be nondisruptive.

The smart commercial energy monitoring system should be self-configuring. It can monitor power consumption in a multi-circuit power distribution system for facilities, such as an engineering lab. The system can be used to identify opportunities for energy savings based on analysis of automated complex power measurements observed on-site and recorded over time.

This system can perform networked sub-metering, with energy use thresholds and alert triggers, in addition to environmental sensing, including temperature, humidity, light, and CO_2. The user interface can show detailed views of circuits in buildings, from mains to branch circuits, displayed by physical or functional grouping.

The technologies needed for are wireless sensor network solutions can be based on the low-power Intel embedded processor. A smart commercial energy monitoring system enabled by Intel technologies would have the following characteristics:

- Intel embedded processor
- Intel chipset
- Expansion buses
- PCI
- PCI Express
- Memory
- DDR2 socket
- Graphics
- Intel GMA 500 with 2D/3D Graphics Engine
- Independent display

- Hardware-assisted DVD/MPEG2 decoding
- Storage
- ATA100
- Serial ATA 150/300
- I/O
- USB 2.0
- LAN
- 10/100/1000 Ethernet
- Sound
- HD audio and AC97 compliance

Intelligence in Smart Home Control Panels

Intelligence in energy is at three levels: smart generation, smart distribution, and smart consumption.

Smart consumption of energy can be facilitated by smart home control panels using Intel embedded processors. These systems can collect and display detailed information about overall electricity consumption and usage patterns for appliances, enabling consumers to better monitor consumption. Such small, intelligent metering systems can be designed with an attractive and energy-efficient multi-function display device that is centrally located within the home.

This panel has innovative user interfaces that provide useful alerts and displays to control devices. Typical computing applications are:

- WSN application framework
- Home control server
- Energy management middleware
- Smart metering middleware
- Whole home media streaming
- Voice - intercom

Requirements of such a system are performance, scalability, enhanced graphics, and standards-based I/O. Graphics requirements are:

- Up to HD (1080i) resolution support
- 3D graphics UI
- Networked video recording (encoding, transcoding)
- Advanced format support : H.264, MPEG4

Other requirements are robust application processing performance, scalability, and excellent graphics performance.

Intelligent home control panels provide solution to such requirements:

- The low-power and small form factor design of the Intel embedded processors enable hardware platforms designed for integration within the home.
- Integrated hardware video decoder supports video-intensive applications
- Smart energy management widgets that to control in-home systems
- Support multiple I/O standards, including ZigBee, Wi-Fi, RS-232/485, and Ethernet

A smart home energy control panels example configuration would include the following:

- Processor
- Intel low power processors
- Chipset
- Intel Low Power System Controller Hub
- Display
- Integrated hardware video encoder - H.264, MPEG-4, MPEG-2
- Memory
- SODIMM DDR2 400/533 MHz
- LAN
- Gigabit Ethernet
- I/O
- COM
- USB 2.0
- Audio
- 1 microphone/audio-in jack, 1 speaker-out jack
- Storage
- PATA HD drive
- built-in 4 GB flash
- Expansion cards
- SDIO/MMC socket
- CompactFlash socket
- System expansion
- SVDO port (optional)
- PCIe slot (x1) (optional)

- Mini Card slot
- HDA connector (optional)

Conclusion

Intel technologies and other industry innovations can be used to create intelligent energy environments. We have seen various ways in which Intelligence in energy can be embedded namely, smart generation, smart distribution, and smart consumption.

5

Intelligent Environments at Home

Innovative technologies like wireless sensors, mobile access, and visual analytics have created the smart homes that have enabled users with the smart control of their homes at their fingertips, no matter where they are.

Introduction

In intelligent home environments, computers are embedded into objects and the environment in order to provide new product-based services to their inhabitants and those who manage the homes. Thus the small size of the Intel® Atom™ processor and its low power requirements can be used for embedded intelligence.

Intelligent equipment such as home appliances and devices offer their functionality in the form of services. Such services are manifested by invisible embedded systems that continuously interact with human users, provide continuously sensed information, and react to service requests from the users.

Significant levels of data need to be gathered from the home environment in order for these products to function intelligently and autonomously. Wireless sensors within sensing devices based on Intel Atom enable collection of data for ubiquitous monitoring.

These large amounts of data have to undergo complex analysis for fusion to get the correct picture of the condition of the environment. Intel Atom's high performance enables analytical processing of this data.

Intelligent homes are always wirelessly connected. This enables all functions to be available as a service. That way all services can be accessed remotely as well as from TV or browsers within the household. Intelligent homes have Web-enabled home appliances and devices, broadband communications, and intelligent products and services. Monitoring and control of intelligent home equipment and devices is possible via Web or telephone. The remote connections to household appliances, embedded devices, and countless sensors need an intelligent networking infrastructure. Intelligent homes can be controlled from anywhere:

- Via smart phones
- Via smart TV
- Via smart home control panels
- Via remote networked computers
- Via Internet cloud
- Via Web browser

The technology foundations that make these possible are sensing technology, computing technology, control technology, and communication technology.

Intelligent environments at home are sensitive and responsive to the presence of its users. The purpose of such intelligent homes is to help their inhabitants be more independent and comfortable.

The intelligent homes are automated since devices are intelligent and work autonomously without user inputs.

Short-range wireless communication technology like radio frequency and ZigBee† enables communications within home.

Many functions can be performed from outside the home due to intelligence in the Internet cloud.

Home monitoring systems are able to do the surveillance and control functions of household equipment with wireless connectivity.

This wireless connectivity enables remote monitoring of home security systems, including anti-theft, anti-gas leak, fire and other functions.

Some of the services provided by intelligent homes are in the following areas:

- Security (automatically sound the alarm)
- Monitoring (remote monitoring of home appliances)
- Message transfer (as in case of emergencies)
- Health and wellness (providing interconnections with medical facilities)
- Entertainment and convenience (smart remote to control the home from couch)
- Energy management (with smart home panels)

Intelligent devices are those devices that have different degrees of intelligence in terms of working autonomously. They can are configurable with rules so they can make decisions and adapt their working. They are also wirelessly connected so they can receive control information or send information about their surroundings through remote communications.

Some examples of intelligent devices in the home are smart TV, smart remotes, environmental controls, smart household appliances, and safety and monitoring devices, smart wellness and smart medical devices.

Typical characteristics of intelligent devices are that they:

- Can sense and monitor changing conditions.

- Provide information about their functioning. For example: a smart refrigerator can report information about the potential failure of its components and ask for preventive maintenance

- Are configurable with rules so they can make decisions and adapt their working.

- Allow control from remote. For example, they can be switched on by external signals when the energy cost is less.

- Provide information about their environment. For example: a smart sprinkler can sense its surroundings optimize its operation.

- Are interconnected and can communicate with people, systems, and other intelligent devices. For example: smart microwave ovens can be detected and diagnosed for failure from anywhere through the Internet.

- Can make optimal decisions based on different data. For example, a utility can send signals to consumers' homes to manage discretionary energy use in order to reduce peak loads.

- Can work autonomously.

- Are wirelessly connected.

Intel processors can be used to power the intelligence in intelligent home environments. They have the characteristics that meet the requirements of intelligence in intelligent homes. For example: Intel Atom–based hardware can be used in smart electrical sensors. Intel system-on-chip (SoC) code named Tunnel Creek can be used for IP phones, printers, and in-vehicle-infotainment systems for cars. Tunnel Creek has an Intel Atom processor core that can be used to create PCI Express–compliant devices that directly connect to the chip. Intel chips can also be used to power wireless networks.

Intelligence is also embedded in form of home energy dashboards that can learn and display how homes consume energy in real-time. Table 5.1 summarizes technologies for intelligent homes.

Table 5.1   Technologies for Intelligent Homes

Technology	Examples
Sensor technology	Measurement of environmental attributes: light, sound, heat
	Measurement of physical attributes: location, speed
	Invasive measurement of physiological attributes: blood
	Noninvasive measurement of physiological attributes: heart rate, blood pressure
Computing technology	Computer vision
	Grid computing
	Cloud computing
	Image processing
	Location estimation
	Security
Control technology	Smart adaptive control and response systems for environmental factors: temperature, humidity, illumination, chemicals in air
	RFID applications
	Smart home appliances
	Multimedia display
	Global positioning system
Communications technology	Internet protocols: IPv4 and IPv6
	Power line communications
	Wireless communications: Wi-Fi[T], ZigBee[T], Bluetooth[T], and so on.

Wireless Sensors in Intelligent Homes

Goals of intelligent homes are communications, control, safety, healthcare, energy conservation, and comfort. The technology foundations that make these possible are:

- Sensor technology,
- Computing technology,
- Control technology, and
- Communication technology.

Intel processors can power all these technology pillars of intelligent homes.

Sensors measure physical quantities in their environment and convert it into a signal that can be read by computing elements.

Computing elements provide analytics to comparing signals and adjusting their magnitudes.

Control actuates smart appliances and personal equipment in an intelligent house.

Communication uses existing wireless standard communication protocols for communication among intelligent agents, smart objects, and so on. A low power Intel Atom–based wireless sensor network (three tier architecture) would have the following characteristics:

- Sensor: ad-hoc wireless sensor mesh network
- Multiple sensor nodes that measure environmental parameters
- Communication: layer of routers
- communicate sensor mesh network data to the next higher tier
- Computation and control: Intel Atom–based server
- Collects and stores pertinent information
- Manages the wireless sensor network
- Provides web-services–based reporting of environmental parameters

Surveillance of Intelligent Homes

Intelligent homes perform smart surveillance in real time by using intelligent remote monitoring and control systems. Smart surveillance systems can send surveillance images and alarm information. They can accept commands from a remote location.

They gather information with a variety of sensors; the information gathered is related to alarm security, inventory tracking, and facility management, and they are made available through the Internet.

The sensors used to gather information can be to measure light, sound, contact, and motion. This multidimensional information about the people in intelligent homes is needed to make activity determination.

However, sensors may not always provide reliable information due to sensor faults, levels exceeding operational tolerance levels, or loss of data in communication. That is why fusion is used to take multiple data from multiple sensors and to derive reliable data from a large amount of redundant uncertain sensor data.

The surveillance information is also gathered using webcams. Security can also be ensured by using remotely controlled locks for the front door and the garage door.

Smart surveillance utilizes networked PCs, video, cell phones, media players, webcams, and Internet phones to monitor intelligent homes.

Wireless and wired environmental sensors can be used for occupancy detection in intelligent homes. Detection of occupant presence enables controls like need-based ventilation and security. Camera networks can also be used for deriving the number of occupants. Ambient-sensing systems, carbon dioxide sensing systems, and indoor air quality sensing systems can be used to estimate occupancy.

The applications of occupancy detection are human-need-based environmental control, security, energy efficiency and sustainable green buildings.

Intelligent surveillance uses automatic recognition of human gestures using computer vision. Gesture recognition also has many other real-world applications, such as sign language recognition and assistive robots.

Healthcare in Intelligent Homes

Intelligent homes can use Intel hardware in a variety of ways to provide healthcare. They integrate information from a wide variety of sensors and actuators. The information gleaned from these elements is processed with Intel processors that implement computational intelligence. Cooperative communication between units is implemented through a wireless network based on Intel processors inside the home; and Internet resources allow linking the home with external services. These external healthcare services IT network is also based on Intel processors.

Intelligent homes can provide healthcare services that can determine the user's health by processing sensory inputs regarding facial, vocal, eye-tracking, and physiological signals.

Intelligent homes can adjust their own healthcare parameters like lighting, temperature, and humidity. By use of sensors and control systems they monitor the home and adjust the various smart devices that provide heat, ventilation, lighting, and other health related parameters accordingly.

Intelligent homes have embedded intelligence capable of sensing the home's occupants and their current state, and providing appropriate healthcare services to them.

The intelligence in homes has context awareness that can adapt and grow according to its location of use, the collection of nearby people and objects, as well as the changes to those objects over a period of time.

Intelligent homes also provide a connected health services platform that captures, aggregates, analyzes, and shares health related data with their mobile devices, PC, and medical personnel.

Intelligent homes connect home healthcare devices through the Internet cloud to the entire healthcare infrastructure. Thus it can also provide cloud-based solutions for fitness, nutrition, chronic disease management, home care, body area networks, remote patient monitoring, and independent living.

Emergency Notification in Intelligent Homes

Intelligent homes can detect dangerous healthcare situations at home like accidents, fall, restlessness, fainting, and running away through individual data collection and analysis of people's movements.

Intelligent homes can not only detect dangerous situations but they can even send emergency information so it flows through multiple distributed interlinked media. The media is intelligent, and is itself the environment. The intelligent media is embedded throughout the natural environment of people. The media is mobile like us and around us, and in part of our intelligent environments.

Intelligent homes send emergency messages smart TV, smart signage, smart Web, smart books, smart radio, smart cars, smart mobile phones, smart GPS, smart refrigerator, smart printers, and to other intelligent homes.

Elderly Care in Intelligent Homes

The elderly and disabled can be monitored in their intelligent homes with numerous smart devices. Sensors can be implanted into their home for mobility assistance and disease prevention. These sensor-embedded intelligent homes can assist people with reduced physical functions. For example, implantable monitoring systems, memory aids, or even assistive robotics help elderly people in intelligent homes.

Intelligence in smart devices has enabled real-time monitoring of the patients, and connects the patient's home to a virtual hospital continuously monitored by health experts.

If the residents in intelligent homes are detected to have increased sleep movement or sleep fragmentation, then alerts are raised to check if these are indicative of more serious conditions. Monitoring sleep restlessness in older adults can provide diagnostic information about their health.

This monitoring is done with unobtrusive, non-contact sensors, to detect rollovers and other sleep disturbances.

Sensor networks in homes provide early detection of potential problems that may lead to serious health events if left unattended or identifying alert conditions such as falls. Sensors can be

•   Motion sensors

- Video sensors
- Bed sensors

All these sensors capture sleep restlessness and pulse and respiration levels.

Intelligent homes monitor human biometrics by various capture devices, such as video cameras and microphones. Intelligent homes keep track of their occupants and are capable of answering questions about the whereabouts of the occupants. Accurate recognition based on biometrics is key to success of such an approach. Some examples of smart medical devices are listed in Table 5.2.

Table 5.2   Smart Medical Devices in Intelligent Environments

Device Type	Example
Noninvasive sensors	Pulse oximeters: measure oxygenation of hemoglobin from fingertip.
	Body fat meters: measure body fat percentage by passing electric current
	Sensor-shirts: biosensors in shirt monitor physiological signs
Invasive sensors	Heartbeat sensor in heart
	Continuous glucose monitoring in blood
	Cameras in pill
Robots	Socially interactive healthcare robot
Health	Smart beds
	Spirometers: measure air flow in lungs

Security and Privacy

Intelligent homes provide the security and privacy of medical data collected by these devices. There is intelligence associated with access control that is embedded in the applications and enabled by Intel processors.

The security requirements of healthcare applications are complex and dynamically changing. Thus, context-based access control architecture is needed to fulfill the security requirements.

Smart Devices in Intelligent Homes

Using Intel® architecture–based processors like Intel Atom, home automation embeds intelligence at multiple levels. These levels are local operational intelligence, user interaction intelligence, and remote decision making intelligence.

Local operational intelligence is embedded in various home devices, appliances, and equipment like lights that are controlled locally.

User interaction intelligence is embedded in logic and user preferences regarding the local home controls like temperature.

Remote decision making intelligence is embedded in the inter-building communications, communications with neighbors, informing about fires, floods, security problems, emergencies, and so on. This includes remote management of the homes, taking into account the optimization of the inhabitants' home preferences, constrained by the available resources.

Smartness in intelligent homes is manifested in two ways. First smartness is about what can be controlled, namely smart devices, like smart refrigerators and smart TVs. Second, smartness is about how these devices can be controlled, namely, they can be controlled by panels on devices, from TV, from a web browser, from a remote, and so on.

Thus we have smart control and smart devices in intelligence homes. Together they take care of various goals of intelligent homes, namely, comfort, well being, security, health, and energy. For example:

- Smart devices can have a security system application.
- Smart devices can have voice recognition.
- Smart automation can involve integration and automatic control of smart devices
- Smart devices in the home can be things like smart lamps, smart fans, smart lights, smart blinds, smart audio, and smart video.
- Smart automation means remote control of smart devices.
- Smart automation means automatic control of smart devices.
- Smart automation can be automation of surveillance or irrigation.

Some additional examples are listed in Table 5.3.

Table 5.3	Smart Devices in Automation for Intelligent Homes
Smart Device	**Applications**
Smart refrigerator	Alerts users to expired items Orders refills of low inventory from grocery order processing system
Smart electric plugs	Can analyze and display how much energy smart devices are consuming.
Smart light	Its illumination can be controlled for safety and energy efficiency. Can integrate information and illumination.
Smart window blinds	Can detect environmental conditions and decide to close or open. Can automatically close at sunset.
Smart surveillance	Home sensors instantly notify alerts on flood, pipe burst, fire, and so on. Ability to remotely check on the safety of family members. Open locks and garage doors from anywhere in world for authorized people.
Smart home theater	Integrated with Web browser and other connected devices like thermostat or environmental controls for customized lighting and distribution of audio.
Smart phone systems	Web, voice, data, and video communications. Can control all the automation in smart homes from anywhere in the world.
Smart irrigation system	Adapts the rate of sprinkling based on rain or heat. Starts all the sprinklers at full force if it detects an intruder.
Smart thermostat	Adapts temperature setting based on weather and sensed household activity.
Smart TV	Adapts recommended television shows based on individual viewing history.
Smart laundry appliance	Adapts temperature and time of washing and drying based on load volume and dirt.
Smart pool cleaner	Adapts the quantity of chemicals based on contamination levels. Adapts circulation pumping and chlorine feed based on weather conditions.

Smart Devices

Examples of smart devices are smart refrigerators, smart washing machines, smart clothes dryers and smart dishwashers.

Smart devices monitor, protect, and automatically adjust operation to the needs of users. They can react automatically to changing energy-rate information. Smart appliances seamlessly connect with other smart devices. For example, a smart dishwasher automatically delays dishwashing to a cheaper time slot. It delays power usage to an optimal time for renewable energy generation, when the wind is blowing or sun is shining.

Smart devices can use radio frequency identification (RFID) for automatic identification. RFID tags or transponders are used to remotely retrieve data about smart objects. RFID tags contain silicon chips and radio antennae. Passive tags don't need an internal power source, whereas active tags need a power source.

Smart devices can be controlled in a variety of ways: local touchscreen display panels, web browser from anywhere in world, home PC application, cell phones, infrared remotes, and TVs.

Smart devices can also send regular reports and send alerts through the same channels. The communications can be binary, ASCII text, video, or audio.

They also have I/O ports and X10 interfaces through electrical wiring for integration with other smart devices.

Smart devices can send regular reports or alerts of conditions like maintenance required, dying power supplies, disconnection of gas supply, or inability to communicate with Internet.

Smart Refrigerators

The smart refrigerator has RFID (for identification), LCD touchscreen display panels (user interface), cameras, and image processing (for recognition) abilities. Smart refrigerators are also connected to trash compactors and sinks for disposal of perishable items.

The smart refrigerator maintains an inventory of items inside it. It can identify items from their RFID (for milk carton) or use scanned images (of apples) of items to identify and report.

It can receive special requests from the user, either on its panel or from a cell phone or with an infrared remote or from a web interface. One such request can be to prepare a shopping list based on inventory and history of use.

It will also keep track of expiration dates on inventory items and alert users to use them before those dates approach or ask users if it can trash them after that date.

Smart refrigerators can also be integrated with the grocery order processing and automatically order refills of items you never want to run out of like, say, Indian cheese and tomatoes.

Smart Electric Plugs

Smart electric plugs go into any wall socket and can analyze and display how much energy different smart devices are consuming.

Smart electric plugs can also wirelessly transmit consumption data to remote hubs. They can also receive control data to turn the plugs off or on selectively in different parts of the smart home.

Users can use a web browser to view data about each smart plug connected socket and turn that plug on or off to cut down energy use where it isn't needed.

Similarly other controls and status checking can be done through a home PC application, phone, TV, or infrared remotes.

Smart Light

Smart light is used not just for illumination but for a variety of other critical uses in smart home environments. It is controllable. Its illumination can be controlled for safety and energy efficiency. Smart light that is controllable can also be used for communications.

Smart lights can integrate information and illumination, leading to multiple uses. They can be used for optical sensing and imaging for detection of accidents in home from a remote location. In an adaptive infrastructure, smart light is adaptable, aware, controllable and efficient. This attribute of awareness is important for surveillance.

Smart Window Blinds

Window blinds in intelligent homes are smart and can detect the surrounding environment and state of other smart devices and make decisions to close or open or partially open or open in an angular fashion.

Smart window blinds can automatically close when certain events occur, like the TV being turned on. They can open when there is a security system breach. They can automatically close at sunset.

Smart Surveillance

Centralized alarm services use sensors and cameras; home sensors instantly notify the homeowner, selected neighbors, or the police and fire departments; the safety of family members can be checked on remotely.

Smart security can recognize specified events and call to alert the users. It can also act intelligently on flood, burst pipes, fire, and water in the basement.

From a remote location (anywhere in world through web browser) smart security allows authorized people to open locks and garage doors.

Smart security can send status and video images upon request or on a regular basis.

Smart security can integrate with others smart devices and turn on in-home lights when the user's car is detected entering in garage. If the person entering garage is an intruder then it will call the police, alert you on phone, and also ring an alarm in neighborhood.

Smart irrigation is integrated with smart security. If it detects an intruder, it starts all the sprinklers at full force, and starts the alarm as well.

Any environmental threshold exceeded, whether it is humidity, temperature, or state of dryness can trigger alarms. Home sensors can also recognize voices and accordingly turn on user's favorite music or favorite TV channel.

Smart Home Theater

Smart home theatre can respond to complex commands with the single touch of a button on a remote. It can take input from multiple sources and send output to multiple destinations, as configured upon certain events happening. This can happen with one button on a single remote and or sometimes even without a button press. For example, when it detects you are in the shower it can play your favorite music video on your bathroom TV.

Smart home theater systems stay invisible and play the chosen entertainment media without any intervention or detailed instructions from users. They are integrated with a web browser and other connected devices like a thermostat or environmental controls for customized lighting and distribution of audio.

Smart Phone Systems

Smart phone systems do much more than Web, voice, data, and video communications. They can control all the automation in smart homes from anywhere in the world. It becomes the miniature computer when needed. It becomes the remote control when needed. It becomes the security system when needed, asking the caller for security credentials before allowing control of smart homes.

Smart Irrigation

The smart irrigation system detects the level of moisture in soil and turns on only those sprinkler zones that need water. It detects rain and skips the scheduled irrigation. It detects scorching heat and doubles the rate of sprinkling.

Smart Thermostats

Smart thermostats change target temperature based on current and coming weather conditions. They have sensors that watch household activity.

Smart TV

Smart TV recommends television shows based on individual viewing history. It recognizes who is in room with biometric identification, greets and suggests based on individual viewer. It also integrates with smart security and flashes the intruder image on TV screen when smarts security detects the presence of an intruder in the premises.

Smart Appliances

Smart appliances like washers and dryers determine water temperature and washing, rinsing, drying time needed based on load volume and dirt level.

Smart Pool Equipment

Smart pool equipment determines contamination levels and automatically dispenses correct amount of chemicals. It adapts operation of circulation pump and chlorine feed to time of day and weather conditions.

Smart Home Automation Controller

Smart devices can be controlled through TVs, touchscreen displays, telephones, mobile phones, and computers.

For example, a single infrared remote control device can do all of the following:

- Dim lights
- Air conditioning temperature adjustment
- Control volume of house audio

Smart home automation controllers provide an interactive interface through (local/remote) TV screen and remote, and through (remote) web browsers, and through custom (local panels).

The following can be controlled through TV screens with handheld remote or from web browser:

- Control electronics
- Control smart security systems

- View status and change levels of security in different zones
- Control smart thermostats
- Reprogram the thermostat schedule
- Control smart AC electronics
- Change the temperature
- Control smart phone
- View the Caller ID information and route calls to other phones
- Control the smart lights
- Change lighting schedule
- Video output on TV
- Display menus and control screens
- Infrared interface for controller interaction with user and with audio/video equipment
- Monitor smart devices (lights, appliances, thermostats, security systems, and so on)
- Battery-backed clock controls events based on time, date, and so on.
- PC interface (serial) for installation, configuration, control, and status reporting
- Web server for control from web browser
- Remote and local
- Monitors for specified events
- Triggers other events or performs specified controlling actions

Intelligent homes with embedded intelligence depend on real-time response to events. Therefore Intel processors can be to provide such intelligence. They provide the required performance in small form factor. Another important requirement is the ability to integrate different smart devices. Intel processors all have same architecture and similar standardized platforms.

Some smart controls discussed above are described in the following sections in more detail.

Smart Control through TV

Smart devices can generate video text for display on smart TV with mini HDMI output for connection to the TV video jack. Multiple screens can be customized to help control smart devices in intelligent homes, including status/control of following:

- HVAC

- Security
- X10
- I/O ports
- Scheduled events
- Flags, timers, and so on

Smart Control through Remote Controlled Thermostats

Intelligent home environments can be controlled by remote controlled thermostats. A cell phone call can be used to adjust temperature of home air-conditioning. The smart devices can trigger an alert on the cell phone if a certain threshold of temperature is crossed. These thermostats can also be controlled through serial or X10 interfaces. Even a TV can be used to program the thermostats on intelligent devices.

Any of these devices can also be used to receive alerts or to checks status or to change modes of operation from automatic to manual.

Smart Control through Remote Phone

Intelligent homes can be controlled remotely via telephone network in accordance with the user's access control profile and a password verification method. Smart appliances can be controlled by telephone touchtone keypad. Also, in case of emergency situations like fire, theft, or gas leak, it sends alarms to the user's phone.

Smart Control through Serial Interface

Home automation smart devices can be controlled by the supplied PC program or any other program or device that can transmit serial data. They can read ASCII and binary data, and take any actions based on it. They can send ASCII text or binary data to control the PC or other devices. They can automatically report the occurrence of any event. Using the serial interface smart devices can communicate with:

- Computers
- Other controllers, like thermostats
- Other smart devices like security systems
- Weather stations

Smart Control through Home Web Server

Home automation can be controlled through a web server. This can turn a home computer into a web server that serves files to web browsers. The control can be done through any web browser, whether on a PC on the home network, or anywhere else in the world. That status of automation can be seen by reports on Web pages. Various smart devices appear as status and control objects into custom home automation custom Web pages.

Smart Control through Home PC Application

Home automation smart devices can be controlled through PC programs that include many application screens. Using these screens the following can be controlled:

- I/O ports
- Macros
- Video displays

Examples of automatic control are to turn hot water in the shower on at the same time as the alarm. Another example is to have the refrigerator print out a shopping list of missing inventory after one press of a button on the remote.

Smart Control through Programming

Programming specifies action to perform when specified events occur:

- Schedules are event-driven
- Events can be enabled or disabled
- Multiple commands and multiple conditions can be used
- Commands are If-Then-Else statements
- Conditional logic
- Flags, variables, timers, delays, waits, macros, can be used
- Power failure: events missed are caught up or skipped, timers handled properly, and timer and scheduled events processed in proper sequence

Smart Clouds

The Internet cloud for intelligent homes is yet another computing paradigm in intelligent environments. In this new paradigm of cloud computing, consumers need no knowledge, expertise, or control over the technology infrastructure in the cloud that supports their intelligent devices at home.

Intelligent devices, appliances, and equipment in intelligent homes can control themselves through automation or can be controlled through the cloud. Intelligent homes make their products (for configuration) and services (for use) available through the Internet cloud.

The Internet cloud is an intelligent and flexible utility approach to services in the network. This approach permits devices to be connected, enabling interoperation and remote access of services.

In the paradigm of cloud computing, all intelligent home computing infrastructure is hosted on an Internet cloud.

The Internet cloud is a common services delivery platform that:

- Contains multitude of computers and servers accessible via the Internet
- Runs applications in a web-based mode (instead of desktop mode)
- Render applications and data is accessible from a connected computer
- Allows the network to become the computer
- Contains elements for intelligent homes and their associated tasks
- Provides user interface, system management, provisioning services.

- Intelligent home services available from Internet cloud:
- Entertainment services available from cable and telecommunications companies
- Content available for consumer electronics devices from the manufacturers
- Smart meter services available from power companies
- Personalized entertainment content available from numerous broadcasters and movie studios with smart TV acting as a portal
- Information about changing environmental and other conditions available from other smart appliances like the washer, dryer, and refrigerator

Smart TV with Intelligence

Smart TV is integrated and interactive and intelligent.

The Intel Atom processor brings intelligence to TV and enables connection to people, to content, and to other devices. It integrates TV and the Internet on one screen. It identifies the user and offers favorite shows and movies, as well as allows surfing between channels and Web sites. Smart TV is interactive with users and enables:

- Streaming movies from Internet-based providers.

- Integrating Internet content, broadcast programming, personal content, and applications, all viewable on one TV screen
- Watching broadcast programming
- Finding and watching television shows and movies
- Downloading Internet applications
- Surfing between channels and Web sites
- Searching online and personal content and broadcast programming from the same TV interface
- Accessing downloadable applications
- Connecting to social networks while watching favorite programs or movies
- Controlling TV with smart remote control or voice commands

- Smart TV based on Intel SoC technology would provide the following:
- Intel's system-on-a-chip (SoC)
- Intelligence, performance, processing power
- HD video and audio
- Advanced graphics for new smart TV devices
- companion boxes
- Blu-ray† players
- Digital TVs

Smart Remote with Intel hardware

Smart remote for smart TV is an Intel technology under development. Smart remote recognizes the user by the way the user holds the remote and uses it. It uses motion sensors to log how users use it every few nanoseconds interval, and based on that, it makes an inference on the identity of the user. This identification of user can be used by smart TV to share targeted messages or to enforce access control restrictions.

Smart Home Control Center with Intel® Atom™

The Intel Processors can be sued to build home control center computing panels. The panel can be used as a central control center for home energy management, control utility costs, access personal messages, and activate home security systems. It can be used to exchange monitoring and control data with smart appliances, smart plugs, smart electric utility meters, and smart sensors located throughout the home.

The configuration of such systems can be:

- Intel Atom processor
- Intel System Controller Hub
- Touchscreen
- Motion sensor
- Video camera
- Stereo audio
- ZigBee for communication with smart appliances, smart sensors, and smart utility meters
- Wi-Fi for communications with Internet devices

It can be used to monitor the performance of each appliance over selected time intervals, alert users to anticipated problems, provide maintenance reminders, and make usage recommendations that can save time, money and energy. Home control center uses include:

- Wireless connection to the electric utility's smart meter
- Intelligent Energy Management
- Proactively manage energy-consuming devices
- At-a-glance view of utility rates, usage and billing.
- Display information about how to reach monthly energy targets
- Clock screen
- Reminder of time-of-day energy pricing schedules
- Smart thermostat adapts settings based on the weather conditions, current energy prices, usage patterns
- Remote management from a mobile phone or PC
- Remote view and control of thermostats, appliances, and security systems

Applications of the home control center include:

- Security systems
- Air-quality sensors
- Baby monitors
- Emergency broadcast
- Video memos
- Email tracking
- Weather updates
- Highway traffic reports

- Trip planning
- Plant watering

The home control center can send proactive notifications to alert users when they need to check in with the dashboard. In the event of a problem, it suggests solutions, such as finding the best available replacement for an inefficient appliance based on usage patterns, energy-efficiency ratings, and utility rebates.

Conclusions

Intelligent homes are intelligent environments that interact with their occupants in ways that improve their lives. The value of intelligent homes is that it minimizes users' interventions and maximizes autonomy of smart devices.

Intelligent homes have the intelligence to anticipate, predict, and take decisions in an autonomous manner. We discussed some of the major application areas, namely health, security, and energy, that will benefit from the realization of smart homes. Smart devices like smart TV, smart appliances, smart medical devices all help build the intelligent homes.

6

Intelligent Environments for Health

E volved medical IT infrastructures and other technologies are needed to enable pervasive information exchange that is critical for medical personnel to make better diagnosis and for medical facilities to improve patient care. The healthcare paradigm is now extended from patient care in hospitals to home.

Introduction

In intelligent health environments, intelligence can be embedded inside every piece of medical equipment, whether they are point-of-care terminals, patient monitoring systems, tiny handheld devices, portable diagnostic equipment, therapy devices, medical imaging systems, remote monitoring devices, wearable sensors, or health-related mobile-phone applications.

Remote healthcare brings all medical facilities close to patients, at all times and at all places—be it doctors, nurses, lab technicians, facilities, small medical devices, or large medical equipment. And this care, diagnosis, and treatment are done in real time, thanks to technologies that mesh seamlessly with lifestyles and user habits.

Smart portable and connected medical devices are worn on the person.

Mobile healthcare enables medical exams in a doctor's office to be extended to a patient monitored at all times at any location for specific health conditions. The miniaturization of medical devices with embedded intelligence allows them to be connected to patients continuously in a practically invisible manner.

Continuous patient biomedical monitoring is done by small wireless sensors. Numerous Bluetooth† wireless biometric sensors connected to the patient can provide critical patient medical information to decision makers at remote locations.

Real time visualization and analysis of patient data is enabled by Intel's high performance processors that allow visual analysis of the large amounts of data generated by a multitude of sensors and presented to medical teams in a cohesive manner, enabling them to make accurate and timely diagnosis and treatment.

Real-time healthcare is provided to mobile patients in emergency since even medical labs are available for remote access, patients' samples can be taken remotely, and using technology advancements, results can be processed in faraway labs. Not only are medical teams available to consult with remote patients on a continual basis, but even computing infrastructure interacts with automated remote medical devices of patients. This communication presents an added piece of patient data for medical consultants to base their judgments on.

Intelligent Health Guide can help monitor patients' vital data like blood pressure in their homes. Intelligent Health Guide can run on a Pentium® class low-power mobile processor. Patients can participate in two-way video calls with their clinicians through an integrated video camera. During the exchange of data, the system protects privacy by using 128-bit Secure Sockets Layer/Transport Layer Security (SSL/TLS) and VPN encryption.

Intel's ever-evolving technologies for virtualization, manageability, and security can enable patient data to be available to medical teams in real time and in a secure manner. Advanced technologies can ensure that these interactions from remote locations are kept isolated from each other for different patients. Technology advancements enable privacy in such sensitive information handling.

Intel's constantly improving low power processors can enable portable medical devices to run for long periods without being tied to sources of power. Intel's small chips have graphics capabilities that support 3D and 4D imaging. Intel's high-performance chips enable patient monitoring systems that track data on multiple parameters from multiple streams and report results in real time. Intel's hardware-based security and remote management technologies can enable secure deployments of remote patient monitoring solutions. Table 6.1 summarizes intelligent health environments and their corresponding Intel enabling technologies.

Table 6.1   Intelligent Health Environments

Intelligent Health Environments	Enabling Intel Technologies
■ Healthcare to remote patients ■ Healthcare to mobile patients (m-health): using mobile technology to monitor health conditions ■ Continuous patient biomedical monitoring ■ Smart medical devices: portable, connected, miniature ■ Timely healthcare with integrated medical environments ■ Smart point of care terminals ■ Real time healthcare to mobile patients in emergency ■ Real time visualization and analysis of patient data ■ Autonomous robots for healthcare	■ Intel's ultra-low power processors enable the portable medical devices that run for long periods without being tied to sources of power. ■ Intel's small chips have graphics capabilities that support 3D and 4D imaging ■ Intel's high-performance chips enable patient monitoring systems to track data on multiple parameters from multiple streams and report results in real time. ■ Intel's hardware based security and remote management technologies enable secure and isolated deployments of remote patient monitoring solutions

Intelligent remote health management technologies move us toward a more proactive care model. Example: smart knee braces are embedded with motion sensors with which physicians monitor rehabilitating patients remotely after their discharge from the hospital. As patients exercise, the knee braces wirelessly send data to the doctor for view on a desktop, mobile, or handheld device.

Remote healthcare brings medical facilities to patients who did not previously have access.

Such intelligent health environments also provide healthcare where there are shortages of specialists such as dermatologists, neurologists, radiologists, critical care doctors, and mental health specialists; to patients living in rural areas, or patients with debilitating illnesses who cannot travel; further, it enables tracking and monitoring of patients even while the patient— or the medical service provider—is in transit.

The low power, Intel architecture performance, and software scalability of Intel® architecture embedded platforms can enable diagnostic and therapeutic medical devices and equipment where a fanless, quiet operation in a portable form factor is important.

Technology Requirements of Intelligent Health Environments

In intelligent health environments, healthcare methods and tools rely on technology advancements. Their ability to provide quality care depends on technology advancements and technology availability. Standards, technologies, devices and applications are needed to address the various challenges faced in doctor and hospitals' abilities in providing quality healthcare.

- Ultrasound, as the most powerful noninvasive diagnostic tool, requires the ability to produce medical imaging in real time based on more complex analysis of multidimensional data.

- Pocketsize medical diagnostic devices like ultrasound or ECG require handheld systems that can run on a battery and are wirelessly connected to the network.

- Medical devices need to perform many functions, some general purpose system functionality like sending email update to billing, and some very special purpose medical functionality like listening to a patient's heart rate pattern changes. This requires systems that run multiple applications like diagnostics, monitoring, dosing, and recordkeeping at the same time.

- Medical devices need to perform multiple functions in their own environments that isolate those functions and their environments from each other. An oxygen level monitoring device in the ICU needs to run critical care functions in isolation from the hospital interaction functions. Systems need to run as multiple different systems in isolation, with different operating systems and different applications.

- Even the miniaturized medical devices should be able to communicate with the largest IT server without having to build customizations for all interfaces. This requires that all different technologies need the same hardware architecture and the communications be standards-based for them to interoperate.

- The medical devices need video analytics and complex computing to arrive at diagnostics, not just point measurements. This needs high performance even in the smallest form factors.

- Most medical devices need to be portable so as to be always available without tethering the patient to a power supplies. This requires ultra-low power computing solutions.

- Medical devices need to be available and working for people everywhere, even in far-flung remote areas. This requires wireless connectivity and needs to be built into the device hardware.

- Medical devices distributed throughout people's homes, hospitals, and transportation have to always be functional, up, and available. This requires systems that can be maintained, updated, tested, repaired, and managed remotely by the healthcare IT services.

- Medical devices need to have improved sensor abilities as they interface with human beings. Most diagnostics are based on detection of changes.

Examples include changes in movement, be it coronary failure or Parkinson's disease, changes in mass and density, as in breast and other cancers. This needs better sensing and communication of sensing data for analysis and fusion.

- Patient information cannot fall into wrong hands. This requires security, integrity, and isolation of data communications and storage.
- Hardware failures must be kept to a minimum. This requires ruggedness in all kinds of physical environments.

Intel Technologies for Intelligent Health Environments

Intel has multi-core processors that offer efficiency both in terms of power and performance:

- Intel's ultra-mobile processors are capable of supporting designs of less than 5 watts. Low power enables longer battery life and fanless enclosures that can be sealed from moisture and dirt. It also provides the ability to make the device temperature in ranges that can be held in the hand.
- Support of standards is important in medical applications, including specifications for sensors, connectivity, aggregation computing, and services, so that solutions can be interoperable and compatible. Intel provides standards-based hardware.
- Advanced platform technologies including virtualization, active management technology, sleep state management, dynamic execution, efficient memory access, graphics, secure authentication, quick assist, and flash disk.
- Small form factors suitable for new medical devices and applications including COM Express, Mini-ITX, ETX, and other form factors that can get as small as the size of a credit card.
- The completely integrated chip, or system-on-chip (SoC), allows medical devices and equipment to use just one embedded integrated chip instead of two or three.
- Intel® Virtualization Technology (Intel VT) in the hardware allows for multiple applications to run on a single platform or device as if they were running on separate systems. It allows a platform to run multiple operating systems and applications as independent virtual machines isolated from each other.
- Intel® Active Management Technology (Intel AMT) allows any networked embedded system to be accessed and managed remotely. This

allows for medical device or equipment to be used in remote home settings or dispersed throughout a hospital network or clinic.

- Intel® QuickAssist Technology allows accelerator-powered computing through an accelerator abstraction layer.
- Intel SoCs have chip-based acceleration engines for cryptography and content processing.

Table 6.2 lists some examples of medical applications and the corresponding embedded Intel processors that would power devices for those applications.

Table 6.2   Embedded Intel® Architecture Processors for Medical Applications

Medical Applications	Embedded Intel® Architecture Processors
High-end imaging Portable imaging Patient monitoring Handheld devices Infusion pumps Ambulance Emergency room Long-term care Patient room Intensive care unit	Intel's ultra-low power processors enable the portable medical devices that run for long periods without being tied to sources of power. Intel® Xeon® processors bring breakthrough performance and energy efficiency Intel® Core™2 Duo processors feature enhanced performance, extended battery life and wireless interoperability. The Intel® Atom™ processor brings the performance of Intel® architecture in small form factor for thermally constrained and fanless embedded applications. Intel system-on-chip (SOC) combines multiple system components into a single chip with easier design, smaller form factors and greater power-performance efficiency.

Intel's wide range of products allows for flexible definition of performance, power, and features. All Intel chips use the same architecture. Hence, software is reusable across multiple solutions. Intel architecture provides scalability and also protects design investment for products.

Intelligent health environments depend on reliability, manageability, and security of medical equipment. Intel advanced technologies—like Intel® Trusted Execution Technology (Intel TXT), Intel VT, and Intel AMT—built into the hardware, help meet that.

These needs are:

- Reliability of computing infrastructure needed for intelligent, networked patient monitors, handheld diagnostic devices like CT scanners.
- Security for safety-critical functions such as controlling infusion pumps or monitoring a patient's vitals during surgery.
- High availability to maintain peak patient throughput levels.
- Addressing worldwide government regulations, such as the Health Insurance Portability and Accountability Act (HIPAA) in the United States.

Medical devices need to be able to

- Handle data-intensive workloads
- Run complex algorithms
- Perform multiple functions
- Communicate via multiprotocol wireless networking.
- Provide secure integration with IT systems

Intel's solution:

- Intel's I/O-rich platforms
- Performance per watt
- Advanced technologies
- Intel architecture provides access to a broad range of software libraries, development tools, and technical resources
- Intel architecture provides true scalability with software stack compatibility and well-defined upgrade paths

Some challenges that need to be addressed are:

- The development of standards for security, privacy, integration, sharing, exchange, and retrieval of electronic medical records and transactions
- Challenges posed by integration of medical devices and IT infrastructure
- Regulations imposed by:
  - Health Insurance Portability and Accountability Act (HIPAA)
  - Standards Developing Organizations (SDOs)
  - Health Level Seven (HL7)
- Support in medical devices for widely used communications protocol stacks, for compatibility and reliable integration with the IT infrastructure, including:
  - ZigBee†
  - Bluetooth
  - Wi-Fi†

Intel provides integrated platform solutions that enhance:

- Security
- Manageability
- Reliability

These technologies are as follows:

- Intel VT is hardware-based assistance for virtualization software that offers the ability to run different operating systems on a single device, allowing divergent applications to run in parallel.

- Intel AMT implements a special circuit in the Intel chipset that can access and control the system, even when the system is powered off or the software is corrupted. This circuit establishes an "out-of-band" link that allows the system to communicate with a management console without relying on the system's standard networking functionality. This hardware-based mechanism enables remote management.

- Intel TXT is a set of hardware extensions to Intel processors and chipsets that can help prevent execution of software that has been tampered with or illegally loaded on the computer.

- Intel® Anti-Theft Technology (Intel AT) for HDD Data Protection is hardware-based full hard drive encryption that enhances platform-level security with built-in encryption and key management.

These Intel advanced technologies work together to bring about solutions in various ways for needs of intelligent health environments:

- Security provided by Intel VT, which allows execution of software in secure partitions. Allows safety-critical code in safe, virtualized execution environments isolated from different workloads and prevent them from interfering with one another.

- Remote management provided by Intel AMT, which enables fixing of equipment problems over the network, rather than sending a technician to the site.

- Trust provided by Intel TXT, which allows a secure, trusted environment with special hardware-based functions that can stop malicious software and hackers from accessing confidential patient records.

- Data integrity provided by Intel VT, which isolates application code and preventing dangerous interactions between different application.

- Consolidation, provided by Intel VT, that allows multiple operating systems and their associated applications in different partitions, so they appear virtually as multiple machines, all on one real hardware system

- Assured real-time performance, by Intel VT, that eliminates contention for resources between real-time functions like processing diagnostic input/output (I/O) from patient and non-real-time applications like the GUI.

- Meeting different time criticality needs by Intel VT, which enables running of time-critical functions on an RTOS and on a dedicated processor core in an Intel multi-core processor system.

- Avoid rebooting the system for failed applications with Intel VT by using virtualization; a software failover mechanism can restart the software running in one partition without impacting the other partitions. By maintaining duplicate copies of an application in two virtual machines, a failover mechanism can quickly transfer processing automatically to the backup in case of an application failure.

- Servicing and troubleshooting of medical devices by Intel AMT, which provides ways to remotely support configuration of systems, updating security signatures and repairing systems when they break.

- Remotely booting a device by Intel AMT, from a networked drive with known good software. It also allows the remote change of BIOS configuration settings, loading of new drivers or loading a new operating system, whether or not the system is running.

- Generating inventory lists of hardware and software components by Intel AMT, for any device that's plugged into the network and an electric socket. This capability also enables IT departments to monitor the software, by version, warranty, and license, of every device on the network, all without human interaction.

- Ensuring each device has the latest virus signatures, by Intel AMT, without user assistance or the device being powered on.

- Automated configuration management and patching, by Intel AMT, helps ensure that systems are protected at all times, thus greatly reducing the amount of downtime due to viruses and malware.

- Intel AMT has ability to maintain and update systems after hours—even systems that are turned off.

- Intel AMT can automate configuration checking and security and software updates, greatly reducing the workload required and spotting problem areas quickly.

- Intel AMT is a set of hardware-based capabilities that enable health IT to remotely monitor, maintain, and repair medical devices. Intel AMT–enabled medical devices allow them to be more readily integrated into the medical IT network and enables management with Intel AMT–compatible remote management tools.

- On-site fixes for broken medical devices such as infusion pumps and central patient monitors.

- Medical device management and tracking activities, resolution of inventory failures and patch deployments.

- Management of a complex electronic medical device infrastructure through standard Intel hardware platform with Intel AMT–compatibility.

- Intel AMT addresses security barriers in the integration of medical devices onto the medical IT network.

- Intel AMT provides out of band communication to isolate, remediate, and reconnect compromised devices through remote network reconfiguration.

- Intel AMT proactively allows push updates and security patches to portable medical devices, even if they are in the "power off" mode, to maintain optimal performance and reduce vulnerability to software-based malfunctions and attacks.

- Discovery, identification, and proactive software updates on assets that are wired into the network and plugged into the wall, even if they are powered off.

- Remote diagnosis and remedial action on devices even when there are problems with the operating system or some hardware components have failed.

- Intel AMT's out-of-band communication channel allows health IT to securely communicate with, diagnose, and repair the lower end devices even if software errors are keeping the device operating systems from booting or responding.

- Devices with malfunctioning hardware components such as nonvolatile storage drives can also be remotely assessed as long as they have functioning motherboards and processors.

Healthcare IT and Remote Device Management with Intel® AMT

Intel AMT allows out-of-band (OOB) medical system management capabilities such as retrieval of asset IDs, hardware inventory information, and Sensor Event Logs:

- Keyboard Video Mouse, KVM-r pass-through for remote console viewing and control.

- Remote monitoring and remediation even if the PC is powered off or the operating system is down.

- IDE media redirection that allows attachment of servers to remote IDE devices for remote diagnosis or provisioning.

- Automated proactive alerts about missing software, high memory usage, overheated power supplies, and so on.

- Remote hardware and software inventory management and asset tracking even if the system is off.

- Security configurations and agents are checked automatically.

- Security patches are deployed remotely.

- Hardware based filters examine inbound and outbound network traffic for viruses.
- Remote power-on provides full control for clinical and therapeutic medical device management. For example: CAT scanners, bedside monitors and point-of-care terminals; cart-based medical equipment like ultrasound with wireless networking; respiratory and infusion therapy devices.
- Remote resolution in case of device deployment failures, application deployment failures, patch deployment failures, audit failures, inventory failures, and security incidents.

Intel AMT remote management technologies enable management of servers, desktop PCs, notebook and tablet PCs. The same technologies can be embedded in portable diagnostic systems, in-room monitors, point-of-care terminals, and therapy systems.

Intel® TXT: Increasing Security with Hardware-Assist

Intel TXT can stop such malicious software from even executing by using hardware-based security features. Intel TXT creates a trusted execution environment, whereby equipment manufacturers and system administrators can define a list of trusted, validated software, and only applications or device drivers on this list can be loaded.

Intel TXT has hardware-based security features that cannot be altered by rogue software, that can run applications in a safe partition, protect crucial platform data, and keep malware from launching in the first place.

Intel TXT puts software and data out of reach of hackers by running applications, operating systems and virtual machine monitors (VMMs) in the highest privilege level.

Intel TXT provides sealed storage in the Trusted Platform Module (TPM) for security codes, like VPN encryption keys, which keeps perpetrators from intercepting secured communications links between medical systems.

Intel TXT encrypts and stores critical security codes and ensures they are only released (decrypted) to the executing environment that originally encrypted them.

Some of the key features of the Intel Trusted Execution Technology (Intel TXT) are:

- Protected execution environment
- Safeguards critical applications and data
- Encrypted keys and secrets (such as platform configuration registers)
- Eliminates potential security holes

- Launch control policies
- Stops compromised systems from booting
- Measured launch environment
- Prevents execution of untrusted software

Smart Health Gateways for Integrated Health Environments

Access to patient-related data is critical to healthcare. Intelligent health environments require real-time data communication between a hospital information system (HIS), clinical information system (CIS), patient smart on-person devices, smart bedside terminals, and so on. These interactions are specified by the Health Level 7 (HL7) protocol standard. HL7 is a health standard that provides a framework and related standards for the exchange, integration, sharing, and retrieval of electronic health information to support clinical practice and the management, delivery, and evaluation of health services.

Healthcare providers can use gateways based on Intel processors and do a real-time clinical review based on data from application servers, physician handhelds, and hospital systems through GSM, broadband, and dial-up networking links.

The medical gateway is an intelligent embedded platform that enables patients, doctors, and other healthcare professionals to monitor, track, and manage healthcare information from remote locations using handheld or desktop devices.

This gateway allows real-time clinical review by automatically capturing vital real data, video, and images from multiple medical devices such as blood pressure monitors, glucose meters, pedometers, and weighing scales available with the patients.

The on-patient medical devices can connect to the health gateway solution through wired and wireless technologies (such as Bluetooth, serial, or USB).

The gateway enables monitoring of clinical vitals, fitness data, and live video and audio conferencing for patient-doctor and doctor-doctor interactions, and collaboration with EMR systems.

These gateways can be based on Intel's high performing processors:

- Intel Xeon family of processors for high performance for complex medical workloads.

- Higher performing cores with greater instruction level parallelism and more efficient overall processing.
- Intel® QuickPath Technology with an integrated memory controller is a high-speed point-to-point interconnect subsystem that increases peak communication bandwidth among processing cores, memory, and I/O devices. Faster access to data increases core utilization, which enables better processing efficiency and faster time to results.
- Shared level-3 cache stores more data on the processor die and brings it faster and more efficiently to the processor cores.
- Intel® Hyper-Threading Technology (Intel HT Technology) enables performance boost. Each core can process two simultaneous software threads—16 threads for a standard server with two quad-core processors.
- With Intel® Turbo Boost Technology, processor clock frequency can be dynamically adjusted to boost performance without exceeding the processor's Thermal Design Point (TDP).
- Native DDR3 memory support up to 144 GB. Larger memory configurations provide performance advantages.

Bidirectional transfer of data between a hospital information system (HIS) or clinical information system (CIS) and patient monitoring devices and smart terminals can be done using the HL7 protocol and other health standards. Other features are:

- Transfer of vital data (depending on the measured parameters):
  - Heart rate, pulse rate, respiration rate
  - IBP (systolic, diastolic, and mean), NIBP (systolic, diastolic, and mean)
  - Temperature, ventilator, anesthetic gas, ECG, IBP
  - EEG, CO2
- Automatically sends trended, vital signs data to almost any hospital chart system
- Admission, discharge, and transfer (ADT) data captured by a HIS/CIS is sent to the monitoring system
- Patient query
- Periodic refresh of patient information
- Periodic output of vital data
- Periodic output of alarm events
- Output of review data, arrhythmia recall,
- Outbound vital signs and inbound ADT capabilities on a single server

- Network time synchronization to the hospital's network time server
- Data collection interval can be configured to the bed level vs. care area
- Back collection if monitor goes offline, such as during patient transport
- Store and forward option if EMR goes offline such as during a server upgrade
- VPN access for remote configuration and support

Smart Point-of-Care Terminals

Intelligent health environments enable hospital patient bedsides to be equipped with modern devices for vitals monitoring, entertainment, and communications. Nursing care can be improved with a bedside wireless infrastructure that helps monitor patient vital signs and track all patient orders.

- Bedside terminal interface with beds to incorporate functionality such as terminals operating the bed, displaying bed cleaning instructions, and showing vital signs captured by patient sensors.
- The installed network also used for closed circuit TV information in the waiting rooms and the hall
- Technologies, like radio frequency identification (RFID), ultrasonic tracking, and voice recognition, at the patient bedside.
- Bedside terminals give patients entertainment with VoIP, e-mail, Web access, cable, satellite, and IPTV companies, video-on-demand, movie rentals, TV, radio, hospital information, event notices, and more.
- Doctors can pull up X-rays and CT scans at the patient's bedside for more informative consultations, helping patients better understand their medical condition and treatment options.
- Doctors can read all patient records in real time such as up-to-date drug dispensing logs. These capabilities require bedside terminals to have a high-quality display and a connection to the patient records database.

Patient bedside terminal technologies:

- Computer
  - o Low-power fanless processing for silent operation
  - o Touchscreen user interface eliminates keyboards and mice
  - o Barcode scanner to eliminate keyboard data entry of medicines information
  - o RFID for equipment and patient tracking eliminates risk of performing incorrect medical procedures, or procedures on wrong patients

- o Ultrasonic microphones to control bedside terminals with voice commands
- Communications
  - o VoIP telephone consolidates data and telephony onto a common network
  - o Wireless connectivity eliminates wires
- Security
  - o Biometric security, such as secure fingerprint recognition terminal logon for doctors

Smart terminals provide:

- High-quality video displayed on a 17-inch TFT touch display
- Bedside client architecture based upon embedded Intel processor with high performance video playback from TV tuner, IP multicast feed, or hard drive
- Fanless design for low noise and high reliability
- Integrated IP telephone that provides telephony services
- Expansion ports on terminal for patient and medical staff peripherals such as keyboards and remote controls, barcode readers, and so on
- Mounted swipe card reader, which can act as a patient's payment device that gives medical staff secure access
- Built-in speakers with optional headphone connection

Bedside terminals with Intel Atom processors (with the Intel 945 GSE chipset) would provide Intel architecture for small form factor, thermally constrained embedded applications:

- Low-power processor that enables small form factor designs
- Cache memory decreases medical image render time
- Integrated graphics and audio enhances the video experience
- PCI Express, USB support, and other connectivity options—a suite of interfaces for peripherals (IP phone, barcode scanner, and magnetic strip reader)
- Wired and wireless connectivity: 802.11 b/g Wi-Fi and 10/100 Ethernet LAN

Intel processor-based smart terminals could feature:

- Intel processor
- Fanless design
- Water and dust proof (IP65 sealing)

- High resolution and bright TFT display
- 5 wire resistive touchscreen
- Rear access doors
- LED warning indicators
- VOIP/analog telephone

The back office IT components that are required to support bedside terminal technologies are:

- Enterprise servers
- Switches
- Security appliances
- Video servers

Back office supports the following bedside terminals functionality:

- Reception and distribution of television and radio channels
- Telephony support and PABX functionality
- Data and information server support
- Internet connectivity
- Security and firewall
- Network management services
- Reporting
- System monitoring
- Diagnostics

Smart Patient Infotainment Terminals

In intelligent health environments, patients stay at hospital, in the same comfort, facility, access to information, productivity, and familiarity as they do at home or in a hotel. Through application of Intel hardware-based technology, patients have the ability to carry out a number of control and communication functions while in bed. This reduces the isolation, boredom, stress, and anxiety that most patients experience when hospitalized. This accelerates the healing process.

Patient infotainment devices are touchscreen bedside computing devices that a patient can use to may access entertainment and education content in a simple and secure manner.

This is an integrated medical solution that provides digital entertainment, clinical services, as well as communications to the point of care.

Patient infotainment terminals at patient's bedside allow patients to:

- Watch movies and TV
- Make phone and video calls
- Play games
- E-mail, Web browsing, accessing hospital intranets
- Alert staff, call for help
- Operate beds, lighting, shutters and other device
- Built-in webcam helps a patient stay connected while she or he is away from work and family
- Connected by wire to the hospital's network, or by wireless broadband for greater flexibility and lower installation costs
- RFID, digital cameras, and smart card readers for data capture and identification purposes.

Infotainment terminals can be used not only by patients, but also by attendants, medical staff, and caregivers. They can look up electronic patient records, lab results, tests, monitor vital signs, order prescriptions, document diagnostic comments, and so on. An Intel Atom–based patient infotainment terminal could feature:

- Intel Atom processor
- Fanless design
- 15.6-inch TFT-LCD with touchscreen
- Built-in 1.3 megapixel CMOS camera
- Built-in microphone, speaker, and headset support
- Equipped with RFID/Wi-Fi/smart card reader
- Built-in emergency key and 2 x indicators
- Multiple input supports: RJ-45, USB x 2
- TV tuner (analog and DVBT)
- Wired remote controller (6 keys)

The all-in-one interactive bedside terminal makes hospital stays easier by providing the same multimedia entertainment and communication choices people enjoy at home, such as telephone, TV, radio, movies, games, and the Internet. The patient experience is enhanced by intranet access, providing them with access to relevant education on their condition, information on their caregiver team, and hospital information, as well as helping them keep in touch with family and friends through videoconferencing, Skype†, and instant messaging.

Patient infotainment terminal also benefits medical staff by providing secure access to electronic patient data with an optimized hospital workflow. As an aid to professional diagnosis, the terminal can remotely retrieve electronic patient records, access databases from the bedside and comply with hospital information systems (HIS) requirements.

Patient infotainment devices makes hospital stays as close as possible to home, office, and hotel environments, with their multimedia entertainment and communication access.

Robots in Intelligent Health Environments

Robots in intelligent health environments take various forms: delivery robots, assist robots, therapy augmentation robots, patient-augmentation robots, and autonomous surgical or caregiver robots.

Delivery robots are used for repetitious and simple fetching such as, for example, programmable drug dispensers.

Surgical assist robots perform routine tasks alongside a skilled surgeon such as, for example, as a scope positioner.

Surgeon augmentation robots enhance traditional surgical performance since they see better, move more precisely, use less space, go faster, and tire less. Examples include robotic-assisted surgery and a guided catheter system.

Patient augmentation robots do things for a patient that patients struggle to do. Examples include elder-care robots and bionics.

Autonomous medical device robots use direct and indirect machine observation plus a model of the patient system to recognize, deduce, and act. Examples include surgery in a hostile environment, technique that surpasses human surgical skill, smart artificial pancreas, or a smart implantable autonomous defibrillator.

Autonomous caregiving robots interact with patients and caregivers to assist in delivering care. An example would be humanoid nurse robots.

Table 6.3 lists some examples of medical applications for robots in intelligent health environments.

Table 6.3	Robots in Intelligent Health Environments
Robots in Intelligent Health Environments	**Examples of Robot Medical Applications**
Delivery robots	Scope holder
Assist robots	Surgeon rounding robot
Therapy augmentation robots	Crutches
Patient augmentation robots	CNC for orthopedics
Autonomous surgical robots	CNC for spine or brain
Caregiver robots	Unsupervised therapy
	Drug administering device
	Advanced neurosurgery path planning and probe guidance
	Artificial heart
	Automatic ablation device that calculates the dwell time

Intel hardware and advanced technologies can bring miniaturization to the processors and complex precise computations, and give the ability to embed powerful processors into miniature instruments. This is important in the area of robot-assisted surgery.

Intelligent health environments can use the robotic advantages of precision and miniaturization for performing various kinds of remote surgery, minimally invasive surgery, and unmanned surgery. Robots can have articulation beyond normal human body manipulation. Also, three-dimensional magnification allows robots to perform surgeries beyond what a human surgeon can see themselves. Unmanned surgeries are performed by surgical robots that are autonomous, who may not even be under the control of a surgeon. Robots are sometimes used as tools to extend the surgical skills of a trained surgeon.

Robots are used to perform minimally invasive surgeries in various ways. Surgeons performing robotic surgery are able to remove the cancer with precision while preserving surrounding nerves and tissues.

Minimally invasive surgeries with robotic assistance have faster recovery, less pain, smaller incisions, early return to normal activities, decreased risk of infection.

With a robotic assistant only small incisions are needed to introduce miniaturized instruments with wrists and a high-definition 3D camera inside the body. At the console, the surgeon views a magnified, high-resolution 3D image of the surgical site. The surgeon's hand movements are translated into precise micro-movements of the robotic assistant.

Some surgeries that are performed by robots are:

- Nerve-sparing robotic radical prostatectomy for prostate cancer
- Robotic cystectomy with urinary diversion for bladder cancer
- Robotic partial nephrectomy for kidney cancer

- Robotic adrenalectomy for adrenal cancer
- Robotic-assisted radical total laparoscopic hysterectomy
- Transoral robotic surgery for tumors of the larynx and pharynx
- Robotic-assisted surgery for kidney cancer, urinary bladder cancer, colorectal cancer, and gynecological cancers
- Robot-assisted minimally invasive coronary artery bypass surgery
- Robot-assisted laparoscopic prostatectomy
- Robotic-assisted hysterectomy for endometrial cancer
- Robotic-assisted extracorporeal continent urinary diversion
- Robotic trans-abdominal pre-peritoneal herniorrhaphy
- Robotic hip arthroscopy
- Robotic single-incision transabdominal and transvaginal surgery
- Remote-controlled vascular interventional surgery robot
- Robot-assisted gynecologic oncology surgery

Wireless Biomedical Monitoring in Intelligent Health Environments

A wireless sensor node is a microelectromechanical (sense) hardware platform with processing (compute) and wireless (communicate) capability. Thus a wireless sensor node has the ability to sense, compute, and communicate.

Intel Atom processors can be used as biomedical wireless sensors since they have small size, wireless connectedness, computing, and communication abilities in a small form factor.

Wireless sensor platform features:

- Very low power consumption
- Soft power switching
- Small form factor
- Light weight
- Connected via Bluetooth or radio
- Integrated MEMs accelerometer
- Integrated tilt/vibration sensor
- Integrated battery

Wireless sensor platforms generally have sensing, processing, and wireless communication capability. They can capture and transfer data to the required location, whether that is a laptop, mobile phone, server, or any other desired receiver. The information transferred is in raw or semi-processed state, making the information usable for further analysis and interpretation.

Wireless sensors are used for monitoring, tracking, or controlling. Wireless sensors enable intelligent environments for various kinds of applications, allowing human health monitoring and providing real-time feedback to the user and medical personnel of:

- Vital signs
- Cognitive awareness
- Gait
- Limb motion
- Sleep
- Gait analysis
- Parkinson's disease
- Epilepsy
- Record fitness and performance
- Improvement of sports techniques

While the wireless sensor node is the building block, it is the wireless sensor network that delivers the complete application.

A wireless sensor network consists of a large number of autonomous wireless sensor nodes that monitor and report upon physical or environmental conditions, such as temperature, sound, vibration, pressure, motion, or pollutants.

A wireless sensor node typically has the sensor, radio transceiver, or other wireless communications device, a small microcontroller, and an energy source.

Unique characteristics of wireless sensor networks based on the Intel Atom:

- Limited power they can harvest, accumulate, or store
- Ability to withstand harsh environmental conditions
- Ability to cope with node failures
- Mobility of nodes
- Dynamic network topology
- Communication failures
- Heterogeneity of nodes
- Large scale of deployment
- Unattended operation

Sensor nodes are like small computers, extremely basic in terms of their interfaces and their components. They usually consist of a processing unit with limited computational power and limited memory, sensors, a communication device (usually radio transceivers), and a power source usually in the form of a battery, or energy harvesting modules, and any secondary communication devices like RS-232 or USB.

Due to the constrained radio transmission range and the polynomial growth in the energy cost of radio transmission with respect to the transmission distance, it is very unlikely that every node will reach the base station, so data transmission is usually multi-hop (from node to node, towards the base stations). Wireless sensor networks are like multi-hop networks. Each sensor supports a multi-hop routing algorithm and several nodes may forward data packets to the base station.

In wireless sensor networks, data fusion is used for processing sensor data by filtering, aggregating, and making inferences about the gathered data. Information fusion combines data from multiple sources to obtain improved information that is of greater relevance. Within the wireless sensor networks domain, simple aggregation techniques such as maximum, minimum, and average, and other more sophistication operations have can be done for reducing the overall data traffic to save energy and also eliminate redundancies.

Intel Atom–based wireless sensors can also be used for electromyogram (EMG) signal acquisition. This allows ability to do analysis of movement disorders, tremor analysis, muscle activity, gait, and posture disturbance, and so on.

Intel Atom–based wireless sensors can be used for electrocardiogram (ECG) signal acquisition. This has applications in event monitoring and recording, atrial fibrillation, premature ventricular contraction, heart function monitoring, abnormal rhythm detection and alert.

Wireless galvanic skin response (GSR) measurements are also done by wireless sensors. That has applications in stress detection and analysis, the measurement of mental effort or excitement, shock analysis, and so on.

Due to their ease of use and flexibility, personal area networks (PANs) of wireless sensors are ideal for healthcare activities in different environments including pre-hospital, in-hospital, ambulatory, home monitoring, and long-term care.

Patients in hospitals are monitored for many vital signs such as ECG and blood oxygenation. These vital signs are monitored using sensors attached to the body and wired to monitoring and other equipment thus tethering the patient with wires. Wireless sensors can give the patient mobility.

The technology solution requires a system that can connect multiple biometric sensors for vital sensors monitoring, such as the following:

- Embedded 45nm Intel® Core™2 Duo processor T9400
- Mobile Intel® GM45 Express chipset
- Separation kernel and hypervisor software
- Intel advanced platform technologies namely, Intel VT, Intel AMT, Intel TXT

Using Intel's hardware platform along with Intel advanced platform technologies and the LynxSecure separation kernel and hypervisor software, the solution can successfully connect more than 25 wireless biometric sensors.

The salient features of this technology solution are:

- Isolation of different operating systems with their own data and resources.
- Integrity by controlling the information flow between these partitions.
- Multiple operating systems and applications: can execute simultaneously with high level of code and data separation.
- Integrated graphics: to support multiple displays by VGA, DVI, LVDS, TV-Out, HDMI connectors, or PCI-Express expansion graphic card.
- Intel AMT for remote management, maintenance and updates.
- Intel TXT for platform protection from unauthorized access.

Patient monitoring systems implement multiple tasks using sensors and actuators for various functions with different degree of safety criticality. Virtualization can improve system reliability in such an environment by isolating different workloads and preventing them from interfering with one another. Virtualization allows consolidation of many applications on a single server.

Separation kernel and hypervisor can isolate and separate multiple partitions, effectively providing multiple functionalities on the common physical resources. This allows multiple dissimilar operating systems to share a single physical hardware platform. Each guest operating system can have its own resources, such as memory, CPU time, and I/O peripherals. Resources are available to each partition, so that no software can fully consume the scheduled memory or time resources of other partitions.

The data security can be enhanced by using virtualization to provide an additional layer of security protection whereby the hypervisor controls memory boundaries between applications.

The real-time performance as the number of sensors and network data rates increase can be enhanced by running time-critical tasks on partition assigned to a dedicated core on a multi-core processor.

Intel VT, supported by embedded Intel Core processors, allows multiple guest operating systems to target the most efficient application. For example, the Linux software might handle the near real time acquisition from the wireless sensors while XP handles rendering graphics and other OTS applications like Matlab or Excel.

Design highlights:

- Intel VT allows RTOS to run simultaneously with Windows
- System capable of running both Intel VT-d and Intel VT-x
- Sensor with Bluetooth radio and EMG sensor pads capable of sensing to 70 mV differential between pads
- Driver for the USB port capable of handling Bluetooth in the RTOS
- System can handle up to 20 radios

Conclusions

We have seen how—in intelligent health environments—Intel processors and chipsets can be embedded inside every piece of medical equipment giving it intelligence, whether they are point-of-care terminals, patient monitoring systems like continuous blood glucose monitoring systems for Diabetics, tiny hand-held devices like blood glucose test meter, portable diagnostic equipment, therapy devices, and medical imaging systems, remote monitoring devices, wearable sensors, insulin pumps, and health-related mobile-phone applications.

7

Intelligent Environments for Transportation

I n intelligent transportation environments, car-to-car and car-to-infrastructure communications help avoid collisions, streamline traffic flow, and optimize carbon footprint of the overall network. In-vehicle infotainment (IVI) systems have intelligent awareness that could recognize a pedestrian crossing the road ahead and warn the driver to brake or use an interior camera to determine if the driver is falling asleep.

Introduction

Intelligence is in the form of information and communications in the transport infrastructures, the vehicles, as well as the remote management infrastructure in intelligent transportation environments. These environments improve human safety, reduce vehicle failures, and minimize transportation times with consequent benefit to overall consumption for a given set of vehicles.

The special feature of intelligent transportation is that intelligent vehicles and intelligent infrastructure are interconnected and interact with each other to fully automate intelligent transportation environments.

Intelligent transportation environments consist of intelligence embedded in both infrastructure as well as vehicles. In intelligent environments, all of these intelligent components are integrated with each other and communicate constantly. Wireless communication is used to tie the intelligence in transportation vehicles with that of the transportation infrastructure. The computing and analysis requirements of such applications can be enabled by high performance Intel processors that are available in all form factors. Most of the information available to infrastructure and vehicle comes from sensors installed in roadsides as well as in vehicles.

All components of intelligent transportation environments are intelligent and well integrated. This brings safety to travelers. The intelligent mechanisms accomplish this in many ways: by providing help to disabled travelers, by alerting drunk or drowsy drivers, with advance hazard warnings, and much more.

Intelligent vehicles and intelligent transportation infrastructure are well integrated with intelligent traffic management for optimal use of roadways and highways, intelligent traffic signals that act on priority basis under different conditions, emergency dispatch systems, and intelligent vehicle location systems. Intelligent lane management and intelligent traffic signal management based on dynamic factors like weather, incidents, and traffic size are critical to a safe and swift journey.

Components of Intelligent Transportation Environments

Intelligent transportation environments have intelligence encapsulated in various forms, such as in Intelligent Vehicles, Intelligent Highways, Intelligent Road Signs and Intelligent Traffic controlling lights.

Intelligent Vehicles

Intelligent vehicles have the following manner of intelligence:

- Intelligent speed control
- Intelligent driver monitoring
- Intelligent collision warning
- Intelligent breath alcohol warning system
- Intelligent navigation systems
- Intelligent environment perception
- Intelligent lane detection and lane keeping
- Intelligent pedestrian and vehicle recognition
- Intelligent real-time perception and sensor fusion
- Intelligent collision prediction and avoidance
- Intelligent vehicle safety
- Intelligent driver assistance
- Intelligent real-time route planning in dynamic environment

- Intelligent sensor fusion for accurate global positioning
- Automatic vehicle localization
- Autonomous vehicle navigation

Intelligent Highways

Intelligent highways have automatic enforcement of road safety, intelligent speed limits and intelligent collision avoidance.

Integration of Intelligent Infrastructure and Intelligent Vehicles for Collision Avoidance

Integration of intelligent vehicles with intelligent infrastructure provides automation that takes transportation safety from passive to active forms by actively avoiding collisions altogether. Smart intelligent devices are used in vehicles for taking split second decisions to avoid collisions.

Intelligent Drive Assistance for Active Safety

Crashes and multiple collisions will be virtually eliminated. For example, steering assistance can be used to avoid lane departures.

Intelligent Traffic Management

For optimal use of intelligent transportation infrastructure, intelligent traffic management is deployed. It operates a range of intelligent systems such as traffic control, incident management, travel demand management, intelligent rail management at level crossings, and so on.

Intelligent Environment Perception to Avoid Collisions

A vehicle's contextual information is generated by multiple sensor data fusion systems used for environment perception. These systems require lots of analytical ability that can be provided by Intel high performance processors in small form factor provide such capabilities. Sensor data from remote sensing devices is transmitted via intra-vehicle networks to the vehicles' electronic control units. This contextual data enables intelligent vehicles to modify behavior so as to avoid collisions.

Driver State and Intent Recognition for Intelligent Driver Assistance

Intelligent vehicles can detect the driver's state and intentions. They can provide driving assistance as needed for safety. Eye tracking technologies can be used to determine the driver's current state of vigilance (such as drowsiness) and driving intent (such as lane changing) from different objective parameters. Image-based eye tracking sensors can be used in vehicles for driver state and mental workload supervision and for intention recognition from look-ahead fixations. For example, when a driver is trying to change lanes and there is another driver in that lane, the intelligent vehicle will actively try and steer away to avoid collision. These embedded devices require high analytical ability that can be provided by Intel processor–based video camera recorders.

Looking In, Looking Out Correlation for Autonomous Navigation for Safety

Intelligent vehicles use computer vision technologies to simultaneously look in and look out of the vehicle. They can correlate the visual contextual information of vehicle interior and vehicle exterior. Thus, driver's behavior and intent can be systematically investigated and image corrective action on driver distraction can be taken. In such instances, intelligent vehicles can do autonomous navigation for safety.

Intelligent Road Signs

Intelligent signs change dynamically for different kinds of weather, different routes, different vehicles, and responsively to conditions like work zone, state of illumination, and congestion.

Cooperative Driving on the Intelligent Highways with Intelligent Vehicles

Intelligent infrastructure interacts with the intelligent vehicles as well as its drivers. These interactions enable safety while driving and dynamic optimal routes and predictable travel times.

Intelligent Surveillance

Intelligent highways have intelligent surveillance and other defensive measures. It can recognize stealth entry of intruders into vehicles, or assaults on lonely travelers. It can do that by scanning and complex pattern matching.

Connected Travelers

All people on road will have information at all times in order to make informed travel choices and options in their journey. Personalized travel information is delivered to them anywhere and everywhere.

Intelligent digital services are available to humans on the road: online bookings, online payments, online parking, online business services, online schedules, online delay and departure information, online forecast of travel times, online directions, online yellow pages, and so on.

Intelligent Congestion Management

Congested routes bring great variation to journey times, primarily affecting productivity but also potentially having implications on driver behavior and associated safety risks.

Intelligent congestion management makes better real-time and predictive information about journey times available.

Intelligent Autonomous Navigation Systems

Dynamic route guidance is based on real-time weather and traffic congestion state. Other services like dining reservation are also provided.

Intelligent Vehicles Communicate with Other Intelligent Vehicles and Intelligent Infrastructure Using Vehicular Networks

Vehicular networks (VANET) enable vehicles to communicate with each other via inter-vehicle communication (IVC) as well as with roadside base stations via roadside-to-vehicle communication (RVC). They make roadways safer and more efficient by providing timely information to drivers and concerned authorities.

Increasing Efficiency with Intelligent Roadways

Intelligent roadways manage traffic on roads in periods of road maintenance, construction, and bad weather conditions.

Intelligent Traffic Telematics Applications

Intelligent vehicles have various telematics applications like intelligent toll collection, intelligent traffic surveillance, intelligent traffic management, intelligent advertising, and intelligent content distribution.

Emergency Management and Transportation Security

Intelligent transportation environments know how to recognize and deal with emergencies. This includes intelligent emergency notification and intelligent emergency vehicle management.

Intelligent Vehicles

Intel processor–based platforms can be used as in vehicle intelligent embedded systems to perform some intelligent functions to ensure safety for travelers.

Intelligent vehicles have ability to receive alerts. They have multiple sensors that monitor the surroundings. Thus intelligent vehicles can receive alerts proactively when collision is sensed as about to happen (passive safety). Intelligent vehicles also have intelligent driver assistance controls that control the vehicle (active safety) to avert a collision. Collision alerts and driver assistance controls for safety include;

- Collision detection and warning alerts
- Intersection collision warning if approaching traffic at intersections
- Obstacle warning if other vehicles or animals are in a vehicle's path
- Lane change warning if other vehicles are in adjacent lanes when the driver's intention to change lanes is sensed
- Lane departure warning if vehicle is drifting out of the lane when the driver's intent to change lanes is not sensed
- Road departure warning if the vehicle is running off the road (from driver drowsiness)
- Forward collision warning if vehicle is too close to a vehicle in front
- Rear impact warning if vehicles behind are too close
- Driver assistance controls
- Intelligent speed control to control vehicle speed based on speed limit communications from the intelligent infrastructure
- Intelligent lane keeping control to control steering if the vehicle lane departure is sensed without the use of a turn signal.

- Intelligent stability control to control throttles or brakes when vehicle instability is sensed

In-Vehicle Surveillance with Platform DVR

In intelligent transportation environments, vehicles can have real-time communication capabilities built inside a digital video recorder (DVR). Fleet management, entertainment, and security can all be provided on the DVR itself.

The vehicle can be tracked through the onboard GPS module and provide security through multiple cameras. These DVRs can be used for vehicles such as buses, cash vans, emergency vehicles, and trains.

The DVRs can be built with the Intel processors like the Intel® Atom™ processor. The DVR has Wi-Fi†, 3G, and GPS communications along with four-channel real time H.264 video capture and hardware compression.

The DVR platform utilizes an onboard H.264 codec chip to convert captured footage into high quality video.

This platform can be built using Intel embedded processors, which utilize less energy, giving off less heat, making the DVR platform a fanless system.

Besides the I/O for the DVR, the platform has both HDMI and VGA video outputs. It has gigabit Ethernet, Wi-Fi, 3G mobile communications, and a GPS module for tracking.

The DVR also includes wide power input range (10–36V) and 12V DC / 1 Amp out to power peripherals such as cameras and sensors.

Other hardware specifications include an internal 2.5-inch hard drive bay, CompactFlash socket, four USB 2.0 ports, two high speed serial UARTs, an RS-485 serial port, alarm/relay, and 1 GB DDR2 memory IC onboard (expandable to 2 GB via So-DIMM).

The DVR system can support Linux† and Windows†, and the SDK includes features for alarm I/O, streaming, RS-485 control, and display.

Cooperative Vehicle-Infrastructure Systems

In intelligent transportation environments, cars communicate with each other and with roadside infrastructure to improve travel comfort and safety.

Intelligent transportation uses intelligent cooperative systems (ICS) and cooperative vehicle-infrastructure systems (CVIS) for continuous vehicle-to-vehicle and vehicle-to-infrastructure communication and services. This increases the quality and reliability of information available to drivers on their traffic environment and makes more detailed traffic information available to road authorities and operators. Both are important in decreasing congestion, improving road safety, and for better use of available networks and faster responses to transportation related incidents.

Open Platform for Cooperative Vehicle-Infrastructure Systems (CVIS)

A single unified technical solution allowing all road vehicles and road infrastructure to maintain continuous communications between drivers, vehicles, goods, and transport infrastructure interact. It is based on vehicle-to-vehicle (V2V) and vehicle-to-infrastructure (V2I) communications. This allows all road vehicles, and the road infrastructure, to maintain continuous communication via a range of media and with highly accurate localization.

This open platform is built on an open architecture and system concept for a spectrum of applications, with common core components to support real-life applications and services. Applications include

- Real-life applications using 5.9 GHz wireless LAN and cellular 3G communication media.
- In-vehicle and cooperative services for increased road safety, efficiency, and traveler convenience
- A power- and space-efficient rooftop antenna unit containing following individual antennas can be used:
  o Dedicated short-range communications (DSRC), wireless channels specifically designed for automotive
  o Global positioning system (GPS)
  o Broadband GSM/UMTS antenna, named CALM 2G/3G
  o Two broadband WLAN antennas, named CALM M5, provide on- and off-road Wi-Fi connections

Intelligent Routers Reduce Cabling Complexity

Earlier, vehicle communications system consumed too much power and required a cumbersome cable, about 5 centimeters (2 inches) wide. Intel Atom–based router/antennas have eliminated discrete wiring for each radio type by turning the platform into a router with five output channels (DSRC, GPS, GSM, and two CALM M5), all requiring real-time processing.

- Cabling complexity is reduced because the Intel Atom processor satisfies the network processing and low-latency requirements of a complex router.
- The universal platform based on the Intel Atom processor connects vehicles and roadside systems continuously and seamlessly using a wide

range of communication media, including mobile cellular and wireless local area networks, short-range microwave or infrared.

- The vehicle-to-vehicle (V2V) and vehicle-to-infrastructure (V2I) communications are based on five in-vehicle radios. For example, vehicles communicate with each other via a DSRC channel, sharing information on vehicle speed and proximity. Vehicles communicate with the transportation infrastructure, such as gas stations and toll booths, using the infrared link. Drivers can monitor their location using GPS, make phone calls over UMTS and connect to the Internet.

- The board supporting the platform is smaller than the prior generation because of the low power and small footprint of the Intel processor and chipset.

- The cabling is less complex since the computing power of the processor is used to implement a router that multiplexes the wiring for the five radios.

- By increasing the information available about the vehicle and its environment, CVIS enables the following benefits:

- Improved traffic safety by helping drivers keep a safe distance from one another, thereby preventing accidents and consequently reducing road congestion.

- Increased efficiency of the transportation system by allowing vehicles to communicate directly with the infrastructure and one another, enabling drivers to make better decisions about their routes with respect to congestion and accidents.

- Improved energy efficiency and better environment by helping drivers choose the most environment-friendly journey, and traffic managers reduce fuel consumption in the network.

Intelligent Roadways

Intelligent Roadways use embedded processor intelligence to manage traffic so as to ensure safety and optimally use roadways.

Intelligent Traffic Control

Intelligent traffic control controls flow of traffic on roadways so as to minimize travel times and making optimal use of roadway capacity. Intelligent traffic control also provides transit signal priority for emergency vehicles and improves safety of bicyclists and pedestrians.

Intelligent Roadways Surveillance

Traffic detection is done by surveillance devices such as sensors or cameras, for monitoring traffic flow and for security purposes.

Intelligent Traffic Signal Control

Traffic signal control coordinates control of traffic signals across networks of roadways by adjusting the lengths of signal phases, taking into account real-time traffic and weather conditions. It also can do intelligent pedestrian detection and light up the pedestrian crosswalks when their signal is on.

Intelligent Speed Limit Control

Intelligent speed limit control posts speed limits on intelligent signs on roadways, taking into account real-time traffic and weather conditions.

Intelligent Lane Control

Intelligent lane control controls the special uses of lanes (like reversed flow) in specific real-time situations like emergency evacuations and construction.

Intelligent Parking Management

Intelligent parking management systems monitor the availability of parking and provide this information to travelers.

Intelligent Toll Management

Intelligent toll management enables electronically payment of tolls that varies dynamically with the level of demand or with the time of day.

Intelligent Crash Prevention

Intelligent crash prevention on roadways alerts travelers of real-time conditions that may result in vehicle rollovers. This is specially the case on ramps or curves. Intelligent roadside warning signs and alerts in intelligent vehicles are used to warn roadway traffic of approaching trains or dangerous intersections.

Intelligent Weather Impact Mitigation on Intelligent Roadways

Environmental sensor stations can be used to monitor air temperatures, precipitation, fog, smoke, or other conditions. Road surface sensors detect the presence of ice and water on the road surface. Weather surveillance data helps plan road maintenance and driver advisories.

Weather prediction of conditions like winter storms and widespread flooding, and forecasting of roadway and atmospheric conditions can help to mitigate weather impact. Additional weather impact mitigation includes weather information services, automatic vehicle location for maintenance vehicles, onboard devices with monitoring equipment, weather-related information for travelers, weather-related traffic control measures such as variable speed limits, roadside winter maintenance activities, and automated weather treatment of the road surfaces and bridges.

Intelligent Tire Pressure Monitoring

Intelligent transportation environments can automatically investigate vehicle conditions such as measuring the tire pressure and alert vehicle owners in case of anything needing attention and thus prevent accidents. Intelligent tire pressure monitoring systems use wireless sensors for monitoring and are wirelessly connected. Intelligent tire condition monitoring systems can integrate with intelligent vehicle infotainment systems, intelligent fuel pumps, and intelligent digital signage.

Intel® Atom™–based Intelligent Tire Pressure Monitoring:

Intel hardware based tire pressure and remote tire condition monitoring systems can be as small as one small strip that can monitor tire pressure across the entire fleet of vehicles driving over that strip. The strip is Intel Atom–based while remote terminals can be larger, more powerful processors like the Xeon®:

- Intel–Atom based tire pressure monitoring strip is attached to the road surface.
- Arrival of a vehicle is sensed magnetically and the impact of each of the wheels is measured.
- A thermal sensor logs the tire temperature.
- Intel Atom–based tire pressure monitoring strips communicate wirelessly to the remote management terminals via the Internet.
- Remote management terminals analyze data of each vehicle.

- Remote terminals send exception and alarm reports to the vehicle owner by e-mail or by text message. Remote terminals print letters that report the tire conditions.

- Remote terminals build a performance record that identify problems such as a slow puncture, tread wear, and wheel alignment.

Properly inflated tires have less rolling resistance, and that reduces energy usage and carbon emissions. It extends tire life with correct inflation pressures, reduces tire-related breakdown, improves on time delivery, reduces CO_2 emissions, and reduces road wear.

As a vehicle drives over the strip, the embedded wireless sensor measures the tire pressure of each tire on each axle. The system can identify specific vehicles through license plate recognition or radio frequency identification (RFID) tag.

Tire Tread Monitoring

In intelligent transportation environments, embedded computing devices are mounted in the surface of roadways. These devices scan and analyze tire tread and other conditions in real-time as cars drive over them. Intelligent roadways capture tire tread depth as a tire passes over specialized grates. The intelligent roadways alert drivers when their tires need replacement to avoid potentially dangerous driving situations. This prevents a number of traffic accidents that are caused by worn down car tires. Drivers are alerted if their tires need replacement via intelligent roadside signs. Drivers can be warned before they enter roadways or highways.

Various components of tire-tread monitoring embedded technologies can be based on Intel hardware. A camera can have a PC with the following characteristics:

- Intel® Core™2 Duo processor
- Multi-core processing performance
- Remote manageability
- Cellular wireless connectivity

Intelligent roadways use embedded products to monitor traffic and improve safety. Sophisticated roadway devices use advanced laser triangulation to measure tread wear. Digital high-speed cameras embedded in the road look up and capture the laser line-illuminated tire surface and record 3D profiles of it.

The camera can be a multifunctional image processing system that enables tread measuring technology. Cameras have been developed that can do image processing fast enough to check tire tread at 75 mph (120 km/h) for innovative traffic safety systems.

The computing required for this high-speed image capturing is carried out by the PC in the camera.

Intel hardware's multi-core computing performance and its robust and silent design plus a wide range of interface options can be used for the image processing system to be integrated into other applications.

A camera-based system can automatically measure tread depth and tread type and can provide the information via Ethernet cable or wireless LAN in order to control warning systems, barriers, camera systems or even road blockages.

Laser diode-digital cameras can fit into shafts in the highway or troughs, tire treads depths can be captured and calculated. The camera system can be implanted in roadways and provide information via Ethernet cable or wireless LAN to activate warning systems, license plate readers, cameras, or barriers. It can send its data via the Internet hundreds of miles away to wherever records are centralized.

Thus intelligent roadways in intelligent transportation environments make roadways safer.

Intelligent Highways

Intelligent highways in intelligent transportation environments use traffic sensors, electronic payment, video, GPS, and other embedded intelligence for congestion-based toll pricing, thus changing the cost model of transportation from static to dynamic.

Intelligent Traffic Surveillance

Intelligent highways use traffic detectors and video equipment to survey traffic and travelers safety. Intelligence traffic surveillance and intelligence traffic control close or open highways based on real-time traffic or weather conditions.

Intelligent Highway Ramps

Intelligent highways use highway entrance ramp meters to sense traffic ramping on the highway and optimize highway travel speeds and ramp meter wait times. Toll rates can be altered based on highway traffic conditions.

Intelligent Highway Lanes

Intelligent highways can sense highway traffic on lanes, detect real-time incidents and accordingly enforce lane usages. Lane management helps optimal use of highway capacity. Traffic lane control can use lanes in either direction, reverse lanes as required or customize their usage for specific events.

Intelligent Highway Communications

Intelligent highways provide specific information on weather, traffic conditions, individual's route, and other critical safety messages to travelers in intelligent signs, custom highways advisory radios, intelligent vehicles, and intelligent traffic lights.

Intelligent Highway Speed Control

Intelligent highways can use a variable speed limit model. The speed is determined dynamically based on real-time traffic and weather conditions. They also can post speed limits on intelligent highway signs.

Intelligent Highway Signs

Intelligent highways can send location-specific traffic conditions real-time information through intelligent signs.

Intelligent Highway Incident Management

Intelligent highways minimize the congestion caused by traffic incidents. Apart from preventive features, they can detect incidents and take actions to mitigate impact. Intelligent highway surveillance detects incidents quickly and helps incident response teams arrive swiftly. They can also capture information relevant to investigation of incident scenes and record that information for later analysis.

Thus, intelligent highways help ensure the safety of travelers through various intelligent functionalities, which can be powered by Intel hardware.

Communications with Intelligent Cars

In intelligent environments, highways are intelligent and talk to intelligent cars.

Highway intelligence is in roadside sensors and roadside units that can act both as a mechanism for the sensor-reported data to be sent out through the Internet or as gateways for the intelligent cars to reach out to the Internet.

Intel technology can bring intelligence to the roadside units and the roadside sensors.

Intelligent Vehicular Ad Hoc Networks (InVANET)

Vehicular Ad Hoc Networks (VANET), provide communications among nearby vehicles (V2V) and between vehicles and nearby fixed roadside equipment (V2I). The main goal of VANET is providing safety and comfort for passengers. Its main features are:

- An electronic VANET device will be placed inside each vehicle provides ad-hoc network connectivity for the cars.

- Each vehicle equipped with a VANET device is a node in the ad-hoc network and can receive and relay others messages through the wireless network.

- Collision warning, road sign alarms and in-place traffic view will give the driver essential tools to drive safely and also decide the best path to travel.

InVANET, or Intelligent Vehicular Ad-Hoc Networking, defines an intelligent way of using vehicular networking.

InVANET integrates multiple ad-hoc networking technologies such as Wi-Fi IEEE 802.11, WiMAX IEEE 802.16, and Bluetooth for easy, accurate, effective, and simple communication between vehicles with dynamic mobility.

InVANET helps in defining safety measures in vehicles, streaming communication between vehicles, infotainment, and telematics.

Intelligent vehicular ad hoc networks (InVANET) use Wi-Fi IEEE 802.11p and WiMAX IEEE 802.16 for easy and effective communication between vehicles with dynamic mobility. Effective measures such as media communication between vehicles can be enabled as well methods to track automotive vehicles.

Navigation systems based on Wi-Fi help locate vehicles inside universities, airports, and tunnels; InVANET can be used as a part of automotive electronics, which has to identify an optimally minimal path for navigation with minimal traffic intensity. The system can also be used as a city guide to locate and identify landmarks in a new city.

InVANET enables cars to communicate among themselves (vehicle-to-vehicle, V2V) and via roadside access points (vehicle-to-roadside, V2R). The integration of V2V and V2R communication is beneficial because V2R provides better service sparse networks and long distance communication, whereas V2V enables direct communication for small to medium distances/areas and at locations where roadside access points are not available.

Mobile IPv6 has special features that provide session continuity and reliable access to the Internet for mobile nodes. InVANET, if built upon on a Mobile IPv6 proxy-based architecture, selects the optimal communication mode (direct in-vehicle, vehicle-to-vehicle, and vehicle-to-roadside communication) and provides dynamic switching between vehicle-to-vehicle and vehicle-to-roadside communication mode during a communication session in case that more than one communication mode is simultaneously available.

InVANET has applications for traffic scenarios, mobile phone systems, sensor networks, topological problems (such as range optimization, routing mechanisms, or address systems), and security issues like traceability or encryption.

Vehicular ad-hoc networks implement a variety of wireless technologies such as dedicated short range communications (DSRC), which is a type of Wi-Fi. Other candidate wireless technologies are cellular, satellite, and WiMAX.

Dedicated short range communications (DSRC) in cars enable vehicle-to-vehicle (V2V) and vehicle-to-roadside or vehicle-to-infrastructure (V2I) communications, while long-range communication needs roadside units as gateways.

Applications and services for intelligent highways and intelligent cars include:

- Rollover warning; border clearance; weigh station bypass clearance
- Fleet management; tractor-trailer matching; transit vehicle data transfer
- Vehicle safety inspection; drivers daily log; toll collection
- Rental car payment; parking payment; food payment; fuel payment
- Rail intersection warning; traffic information; traveler information
- Vehicle registration; diagnostic data transfer; repair service record
- Emergency vehicle warning; cooperative collision warning
- Adaptive headlight aiming; adaptive drive train management
- Merge assistant; point-of-interest notification; curve speed warning
- Highway/rail collision warning; animal crossing zone information
- Low bridge warning; work zone warning; stop sign warning
- Wrong-way driver warning
- Infrastructure intersection collision warning
- Pedestrian/children warning; school zone warning
- Stop sign movement assistance; traffic signal warning

- Low parking structure warning; pre-crash sensing
- Intersection collision warning; curve speed warning
- Visibility enhancer; electronic brake lights; blind merge warning
- Post-crash warning; lane change assistant; left turn assistant
- Stop sign movement assistant; cooperative glare reduction
- Blind spot warning; infrastructure-based traffic probes
- Post-crash warning
- Intelligent on-ramp metering
- Intelligent traffic lights

Intelligent highways learn about traffic accidents from roadside sensors and other vehicles and alert your car. They also calculate alternate routes to help you arrive safely.

The intelligent highways system that use Intel technologies can have:

- Energy-efficient processors
- Wireless sensors and gateway servers
- Communications for in-vehicle systems

Highway traffic management, accident prevention, roadway weather management, traffic emergency management, traveler information, and ecologically beneficial trip planning are some of the applications of intelligent highways.

Intelligent transportation systems (ITS) is a set of intelligent, connected solutions combining wireless communications and energy-efficient computing technology with highway infrastructure, vehicles, and drivers.

- It collects traffic flow and road condition data using detectors in RSU devices, consisting of sensors and wireless gateway servers, located at regular intervals along the highway's edge.
- The RSUs share data through machine-to-machine (M2M) communications with in-vehicle systems and regional servers connected through wireless links, such as 3G or Wi-Fi.
- Sensors can also be mounted in each vehicle, streaming real-time data on speed and road conditions to the nearest RSU, which can analyze the information for transmission to following vehicles, intelligent road signs, or automated highway advisory radio systems.
- RSUs connected to electronic warning signs can trigger alerts delivered through in-vehicle infotainment (IVI) systems to warn drivers that their speed is too high as they approach curves.

- Collision warning sensors at intersections can communicate with in-vehicle systems to alert drivers to the presence of approaching vehicles, bicycles, or pedestrians. Road monitoring can also issue driver advisories concerning ice, wet pavement, and other weather conditions.

Embedded Intel Atom processors provide scalable, energy-efficient performance needed for roadside units (RSU), as well as antenna systems and sophisticated human-machine interfaces (HMI) inside vehicles.

Embedded Intel processors can be used in RSU gateways, in vehicles, and in highway management servers provide consistent platform architecture.

Other applications can include speed control to help avoid accidents, video-based collision reporting, automated electronic calling systems connected to emergency response agencies, speed management for traffic calming, as well as traveler information and route planning assistance.

Monitoring with Wireless Sensor Networks

In intelligent transportation environments, multiple wireless sensor networks (WSNs) perform real-time monitoring. Wireless sensor networks can be characterized as follows:

- Wireless sensor nodes are IP- and Web-enabled devices distributed in faraway buildings
- A WSN router enables communication with any number of wireless sensors across the network
- Internetworking is possible between server-hosted applications and WSNs
- Connects over LAN or WAN links to a server, which translates embedded sensor applications into web services and web-based applications
- Connects over short-range, low-power IEEE 802.15.4 radio to sensor nodes
- Management services can reside in remote data center

These WSNs can be used to provide information of the location of each railcar, its operating condition, or parameters affecting the cargo. The benefits of such real-time monitoring of railways are that greater speed and reliability can be assured. The sensor networks also provide proactive information for preventative maintenance for railways.

Networked sensors can be used to monitor the vibration patterns and temperature of railcar wheel bearings. This has great value since wheel bearing condition is a key determinant of the speed at which trains can be operated, and that preventive maintenance can help railways reduce the incidence of wheel bearing failure, one of the leading causes of train derailments.

Not just the condition of railcars, but the integrity of perishable and environmentally sensitive cargo is also be monitored.

Networked sensors are used for wireless detection of temperature, humidity fluctuations, mechanical shock and the security of the car and its contents.

Networked sensors are used for detection of proximity data that can be used for anti-collision and automatic braking systems.

Hardware for Monitoring Rail Cars:

These wireless sensor networks and gateway devices that provide tracking data in railway cars can be based on Intel Atom processors. The hardware is based on a new generation of low power, long life, and resilient embedded components.

The special capabilities of Intel processors that can be used for wireless sensor networks as well as gateways are local data processing and storage, low power, fanless design, and IEEE 802.15.4 radio wireless connectivity.

Sensors wirelessly connect via radio with an embedded router device that handles intra-car data processing and storage, network and power management, and routing of secure inter-car communications.

Each router is a multi-protocol wireless computing platform with an Intel Atom processor, memory, storage, I/O, and radio components optimized for long life and low power.

These on-railcar devices also communicate via Wi-Fi with handheld mobile devices that enable railroad personnel to query historical data from onboard storage to check on conditions within each car.

The gateway server is also on the rail and has an embedded Linux and multi-core Intel processor. This server runs web services applications. It also performs network management of the inter-car mesh network created by the railcar routers, manages database storage, and integrates with external enterprise systems using a wide area network technology such as 802.15.4 or Wi-Fi.

Wireless sensor networks provide distributed sensing of physical conditions in real time, based on mesh network technology. Based on distributed application architecture, mesh networks are multi-hop, self-configuring, self-healing, and capable of dynamic routing.

Each railcar includes tiny wireless sensors partially powered by the vibration of the car itself, a process known as parasitic power harvesting. Each sensor can operate on as little as 20 milliamps of electrical current.

IP-based wireless sensor networks have many applications in environmental monitoring, energy supply continuity and optimization, intelligent grid operations, emergency response, rail transportation, retail asset tracking and wayside services.

A WSN router can be used as connection between data center residing servers and in field sensors. Sensor applications can be put in protected and highly available data centers, while sensor nodes and networking functions can be distributed as needed in faraway buildings. The router can connect over short-range, low-power IEEE 802.15.4 radio to multiple sensor nodes.

This network scenario of usage in railcars utilized innovative component architecture, networking protocols, an ultra-low power embedded Intel Atom processor with power efficiency algorithms, parasitic power harvesting capabilities, and on-railcar power generation. It also utilized embedded multi-core Intel processors that support real-time and open source operating systems for management of the wireless sensor network, data collection, and communication.

With wireless sensor networking built within rails we come closer to the intelligent environments consisting of pervasive, fine-grained network sensing.

Intelligent Transport Environment Challenges

ITS information management supports the archiving and retrieval of data generated by other ITS applications and enables ITS applications that use archived information. Decision support systems, predictive information, and performance monitoring are some ITS applications enabled by ITS information management. In addition, ITS information management systems can assist in transportation planning, research, and safety management activities.

Real-Time Alerts for Safety While Driving

Multiple sensors capture basic real time parameters and raise real-time alerts in case of danger. The challenge is to ensure the alerts are in much in advance so mishaps can be avoided. Need to quantify the danger level of the situation, and define threshold of alerts above which the situation becomes dangerous.

Preventing Pedestrian Hits on Roads

The challenge is to detect pedestrians by extracting moving objects from their background. Intelligent fusion of visual sensor inputs is required.

Inter-Vehicular Communications for Different Applications

Solutions designed for specific applications cannot directly extend to general context applications for inter-vehicular communication. Inter-vehicular communications architectures are needed that allow the deployment of a wide set of possible applications from road safety to entertainment.

Intelligent Traffic Signal Real-Time Analysis

Traffic signals need to make real-time optimal decisions for dynamically changing conditions. They can use genetic algorithms for the optimization and simulators for evaluating every possible solution for traffic light programming times.

Intelligent Traffic Management Is Critical for Safety and Efficiency

Intelligent traffic management uses dynamic traffic management and intelligent infrastructure technologies in order to optimally use the existing infrastructure and reduce bottlenecks. Mobile technologies enable the collection of data from distributed, moving vehicles in real time for analysis and assessment of traffic flows.

Challenge: to accurately forecast travel times for route optimization. Accurate traffic flow predictions based on volume patterns of past are necessary to provide intelligent traffic control with optimal results.

Challenge: to keep track of real-time conditions on highway routes for real time traveler information.

Challenge: to control the flow of vehicular traffic through crossroads to reduce traffic jams. Vehicle-to-vehicle wireless communication can be used to determine the position and speed of vehicles in the traffic environment around a crossroad. Thus intelligent vehicles can calculate the optimal speed to maximize the number of cars driving through the intersection.

Challenge: to ensure smooth transit in spite of all issues of large-sized vehicle restrictions for bridges, tunnels, steep gradients, and congested or environmentally sensitive areas.

Challenge: to take into account real-time weather and seasonal effects for effective flow of traffic. Indicators and quantifiers of transport efficiency, journey time reliability, and network efficiency are also needed for analysis of optimal routes. Real-time travel time prediction methods and increased reliability of short-term traffic forecasting models are needed.

Challenge: to create dynamic traffic management and control models utilizing embedded information and real-time data transmitted from the vehicles about position, speed, origin, and destination.

Challenge: to have more automation in traffic flow control to provide routes as well as access to routes, lanes, and parking. Real-time traffic management needs to be integrated with real-time traffic restrictions, road conditions, and parking availability for reliable travel time prediction and optimal route selection. Assessment tools are needed for traffic management strategies, based on dynamic capacity optimization models, taking into account dynamic lane allocation and electronic parking management services.

Challenge: to do intelligent, dynamic lane allocation taking into account variable lanes and speed limits for different traffic flows and different types of vehicles.

Challenge: to do dynamic mobility and traffic management on special events, planned or unanticipated.

All these need deeply analytical computation in small form factors with minimal power requirements that can be easily fulfilled by Intel processors.

Intelligent Transportation Surveillance

Intelligence transportation systems needs surveillance technologies to deter and respond to road accidents, crimes in roadways and vehicles, suspicious activities of individuals, groups or their belongings, and terrorism. Visual surveillance requires analytical models in image processing. This includes suspicious behavior, recognition of a single traveler such as loitering, multiple traveler interactions such as attacks, traveler-vehicle interactions such as vehicle theft, and traveler and location interactions (objects left behind). This also includes real-time detection of vehicle license plates with high definition surveillance video analytics.

Accurate Localization

Accurate localization is needed for applications such as parking slot identification, lane keeping, distance relative to other vehicles based on vehicle-vehicle and vehicle-infrastructure communications.

Autonomous Guidance in Intelligent Navigation

Intelligent navigation systems are autonomous. Challenge: to do automatic vehicle guidance with full control of speed and distance management systems so as to increase road capacity controlled by multiple intelligent navigation systems in different intelligent vehicles.

Intelligent Vehicle Communication with Telematics

Challenge: to develop communication systems for real-time information transmission between the infrastructure, vehicles, and travelers for monitoring, maintenance and operating activities for the infrastructure. The communication systems also need to support management and processes for emergencies. Communications avoidance or reduction of congestion will contribute to improved safety.

Conclusion

We have seen how Intel processors can be used for enabling intelligence in all parts of intelligent transportation components; intelligent roadways enable dynamic traffic management; allowing dynamic allocations of lanes, intelligent merging systems, speed control, guidance systems, and lane prioritizing for emergency vehicles.

Most analysis tools to meet different challenges need greater computing power in the smallest form factors. Genetic algorithms for optimization, image processing for recognition, visual analytics for surveillance, cluster computing for fault tolerance, simulators for intelligent decisions, and so on need Intel processors in their smallest form factors.

8

Robots at Our Service

A characteristic of the intelligent environments is the prevalence of autonomous robots everywhere. These autonomous robots can be found as robot farmers, robot tractors, service robots, and so on.

Introduction

Robots are no longer autonomous entities that learn and adapt themselves to a world made for humans. In intelligent environments, robots interact with devices distributed throughout the environment and get across heterogeneous information by means of communication technologies.

Service robots will enrich all parts of people's lives and be the foundation of intelligent environments. They will help us perform tasks that are dangerous, dirty, repetitive, or remote. Personal service robots will become such an integral part of our lifestyle that it will be difficult to imagine our life without them. Specialized robots will be used in every field including medicine, space, agriculture, firefighting, hotels, and entertainment.

Unlike traditional industrial robots performing repetitive tasks inside protective laser curtains, service robots will interact with people in natural environments to perform various services. Service robots will add to the comfort of human beings. The adoption will first be among tech-savvy individuals but will increase as people see the value of service robots.

The computing trends of today namely, the smaller size, higher performance, ruggedness, and standardization have brought this closer to reality. Service robots will evolve from today's robots. They will share common general purpose robot building platforms, but will have vastly different areas of expertise.

The characteristics of service robots are:

- Perform services for humans
- Sensors, control systems, manipulators, power supplies, and programming
- Autonomous operation
- Flexible, robust, and agile motion
- Movement: rolling on wheels, walking on legs, propelled by thrusters
- Physical mobility: climb stairs, negotiate rock piles, and plow through snow
- Intelligence: programmed; self-learning
- Intuitive: easy to operate and control with little or no training.
- Sensors: environment awareness: light, touch, pressure, chemical, sonar, taste
- Situational awareness: color cameras with night vision, thermal, and zoom
- Energy: solar, electrical, battery; long battery life
- Easy to maintain and sustain; rugged and retrievable
- Easily transportable; ready for operation
- Fast response time
- Reusability: for example, able to withstand repeated decontamination
- Collaboration: multiple robots communicate, coordinate, and work together to handle large or complicated tasks

Nature-Inspired Robots

Robots engineered after biological systems will mimic animals with smart engineering and machine learning.

Underwater diagnostic robots can monitor wildlife to track biodiversity or inspect oil drilling operations to monitor or prevent leaks. They travel efficiently by mimicking the movements of a shark.

Flying robots can be used for everything from indoor surveillance to exploring collapsed buildings. By mimicking bats the robots would be is capable of maneuverability while flying.

Similarly, climbing robots can scale smooth vertical surfaces emulating lizards.

Robotic cars mimic fish to drive in a fleet without bumping into each other. They can travel closely yet can quickly switch direction, like a school of fish. To avoid crashes they measure the distance between obstacles using laser rangefinders.

Robotic service dogs can assist visually impaired or motor impaired people. Their vision systems mimic the key visual functions of the human brain. They can maneuver quickly and safely through cluttered environments.

Robot rats can seek out and identify objects using whiskers, just like real rats.

Snake robots can slither into holes and narrow places to do inspections.

Humanoids

For applications requiring natural and intuitive human interaction with robots, we will create humanoid robots modeled after us. This will facilitate operation in environments meant for people. Modeled after the human body, these robots will look like humans. They will be bipedal, just as tall as us. They can even jump and land by emulating the human musculoskeletal system.

They will also replicate human behaviors and emotions. They can speak, and comprehend spoken languages. They can find their way around homes and cities, and talk to strangers. They learn to make realistic facial expressions, like smiling, by interacting with the people around it. They recognize gestures; and shakes hands when it sees a gesture of handshake from another. It can recognize environment and sound. They can recognize facial gestures like a nod or rolling of eyes.

Some, like robotic personal butlers, will be designed as personal companions to assist people at home. These programmable robots will allow developers to implement their own robotics applications for assistance. They can integrate with user's home network system, greeting visitors and informing residents of arriving visitors. They can provide companionship, or news and weather updates. They can clean homes, using elevators or stairs to travel between floors.

Robotic waiters and bartenders will provide hospitality outside the home. These life-sized robots will stand and walk, and take complicated instructions or orders. They will contain human-like joints, cameras and sensors to avoid obstacles, and Wi-Fi† for remote control over the Web. They have freely moving ability and flexible hands, which make them a special assistant. They have distant voice recognition using microphones. They have environment recognition, can generate maps generation, and localize using a scanning rangefinder. Their obstacle evasion technology provides safe maneuvering between moving objects. They can navigate through corridors, around obstacles, weave between moving people, guide visitors to their destinations, and deliver drinks and documents.

Robot avatars or surrogates in the work or hospital will allow the next level of personal telepresence beyond the computer screen.

Robot Vehicles

Autonomous vehicles will be used for transportation, security, and search and rescue. They will provide high-speed mobility, maneuverability, and reliability on any terrain and environment. They learn to autonomously navigate any environment, and detect objects of interest such as people and vehicles. Using machine learning, they can adjust strategies, acquire new capabilities, and continuously adapt to surroundings. Since they require no human intervention, they can operate for much longer in a greater range of environments and conditions than manned vehicles.

Robot driven cars will provide guidance, safety, and convenience in vehicle travel. They will perform complex traffic maneuvers without human assistance, such as merging, passing, parking, avoiding obstructions, and negotiating intersections. By communicating with neighboring vehicles, these cars will make more efficient use of the roadways than their human driven counterparts. Smaller versions will shift people between different gates and terminals of airports.

For security, autonomous cars or airplanes can observe and monitor large areas from the ground or the sky. Unmanned aerial vehicles, ships, and trucks can transport large payloads across land, sea, sky, or into space.

Search and rescue robots of different sizes and capabilities can be an invaluable aid to rescue workers. Swarms of tiny communicating robots can divide and conquer difficult search problems, like finding survivors after a disaster. Larger robots can reach or rescue survivors of urban earthquakes or mining accidents.

Sentry Robot

Robotic surveillance can provide unmanned, unattended, remote security and surveillance capability. It can also do remote threat assessment capability allowing appropriate response.

An automated Robot sentry can verify inventory, detect intruders, and check gates as part of a complete security system that includes fixed detection capabilities and human security guards.

It provides unmanned, unattended, remote security and surveillance capability. It can also do remote threat assessment capability allowing appropriate response.

It can have real-time obstacle avoidance systems that enable it to share the road with other vehicles. Capable of detecting a walking, crawling, or running intruder at highway speeds. They complete its scheduled patrol missions autonomously, randomly varying its path along the patrol.

Robotic house-sitters can roll around your home on wheels, using infrared sensors to detect suspicious movement and a video camera to transmit images to absent residents. These robots can also automatically dust and mop floors, automating floor cleaning and security in one.

Sentry Robots also come as huggable robot toys that are fitted with sensors.

A robot teddy can interact with its owner and could alert medical staff to changes in a sick child's condition. The robot teddy responds to cuddles and recognizes its owner as they approach it. It can be a companion for children and older people. Robot teddy raises the alarm if its owner is in distress.

Robots in Dangerous Places

Remote controlled robots can protect human first responders and the community from danger. Firefighter robots can enter and extinguish burning buildings. SWAT robots can provide surveillance and protection with fewer fatalities. Ordinance disposal robots can help bomb squads perform dangerous bomb disposal. Surveillance and reconnaissance robots will evaluate dangerous scenarios like hostage situations, giving first responders a tactical advantage.

Dangerous routine jobs, like underground mining or deep sea oil exploration, can also be performed by robots. For example, robots are used in deep-water oilrigs to help with the operation and maintenance of the oilrig. They can dive into the sea and carry out the necessary repairs to the leaking pipe or broken cable or a leaking ship. These reduce the risk to the remote human operator and the probability of human error.

Rovers, or continuous robot explorers, can go places humans can't. Underwater rovers or robotic gliders can withstand the pressures of the oceans to provide new knowledge about marine protected areas, harmful algal blooms, or oil spills. Space rovers can collect samples, take pictures, and transmit back data.

Robots can help us with inspection and repair of dangerous, difficult hazardous, lethal or hostile environments. Inspector robots can be used for fuel storage tank inspections, pipeline and sewer inspection, subsea inspection, and confined spaces inspection. For example, snake robots are used to inspect pipes in nuclear reactors; a snake robot can be mounted on a mobile vehicle used to inspect complex pipework and structures within reactors. The snake robots are equipped with tip cameras for pipe inspection. Snake robots can be controlled safely from remote locations; they can sneak through cracks and into buildings, and send back sound and video of its environments in real time.

Subject robots can be used for toxic chemical testing. Use of subject robots for testing allows testing potentially hazardous chemicals on cells grown in a laboratory, without using live animals.

Robots on the Farm

Sensing robots use GPS to determine where they are within a field and provide accurate measurements at specific locations. Farmers can get precise real-time data on fertility, pests, crop diseases, and soil moisture to measure and improve yield and quality.

Precision farming robots can use the sensor data to accurately deliver pesticide and fertilizer where needed. Hoeing robots can respond with nonchemical means, reducing the need to use herbicides. They sow seeds and other harvesting depending on soil analysis.

Autonomous farming robots use a vision system to distinguish weeds from crops. They are capable of following the edge of crops using touch or ultra-sound sensors. They also use sensors to monitor their own performance and make adjustments where necessary.

Picking robots with laser signals to orient themselves can navigate around a field or greenhouse. They identify, pick, and accurately grade apples, packing them with fruit of similar grade.

Plant sorting robots use computer vision and machine learning to inspect and grade harvested strawberry plants and then mechanically sort them by quality—tasks that until now could only be done manually.

Robots perform other specialized tasks like sheep shearing, crop scouting, grain feeding, weeding, and spraying.

Robotic Human Augmentation

Retinal chip implants provide bionic eyes for aiding vision. They create the sensation of seeing light by electrical stimulation of the remaining working retinal cells still have photoreceptors. By electrically stimulating the retina by a pattern of electrodes, bionic eyes recreate the visual scene.

Bionic hands with life-like bionic fingers will be operated naturally with myoelectric controls. They pick up electrical signal generated by muscles in the remaining portion of the patient's limb using electrodes sitting on the surface of the skin.

Bionic legs will help patients with neuromuscular damage due to stroke, multiple sclerosis, Parkinson's disease, osteoarthritis, or past knee surgery. Multiple sensors detect the user's actions, such as sitting or climbing stairs. Embedded processors on the device analyze this information and transparently apply the force needed to augment the user's actions.

Intensive therapy with robots can even help stroke patients regain natural limb movement after a stroke.

Exoskeleton robots can augment human performance by providing external skeleton support. These robotic suits will be worn by a person to increase strength, speed, and endurance. One application may be for rescue workers inside collapsed buildings, to provide strength to lift heavy debris while protecting workers from falling rubble. These robots will include a power supply to provide activation-energy for limb movement, and some will include legs, torso and arms that mimic human movement using complex kinematics.

For therapy, exoskeleton pediatric robots can be used for intensive locomotion therapy of children with neurological disorders.

Robot Swarms in the Blood Stream

Robot swarms are inspired by ant swarms. Their collaborative action is also inspired by chains of events that lead to fertilization between the one of countless sperms and the egg.

Micro- or nano-robots are injected into the blood and swim in our blood stream to diagnose deadly diseases, deliver drugs locally, and cleanse the blood stream of contaminations.

They are so tiny that they can get into the tiniest places or be dispersed in their millions.

They are harmless and driven by intelligence and a sense of purpose. Once their purpose is done they leave the blood stream.

Each tiny robot by itself cannot complete the overall mission, but by shared communication between countless robots of the swarm, there is a coherent and collective delivery of the overall purpose.

They can swim in the blood, they can measure the internal pressure of blood and of vessels, and they can do the local malignant cell treatment.

For example, a robot swarm can look for a microbe in the blood stream. When any one robot finds the microbe, it locks onto it. It then releases a molecule that diffuses away the rest of robot swarm. It can then release a chemical payload, or mix two chemical reactants from different compartments itself. They do controlled precise delivery of a drug to the place where it is needed, rather than dosing the whole body.

Surgical Robots

There is a need to perform delicate surgical procedures safely in tight spaces where the surgeon cannot see directly. Robotic devices that use technologies like imaging, sensing, mechatronics, and machine vision assist surgeons.

Laparoscopic surgery through a tiny incision offers quicker surgeries, minimal blood loss, decreased length of hospital stays, a reduction in surgical complications, and reduced recovery times. However, it is difficult because surgeons must work with long slender instruments that provide little feedback, and have a limited view of the operating area through a single camera.

Robot-controlled endoscopic cameras allow surgeons to more accurately see inside patients. Robot arms can be more precise without error, hesitation, or need to pause. They can be controlled with intuitive motion and fingertip controls to provide motion scaling and tremor reduction. These robots provide surgeons with natural dexterity and full range of motion for precise operation through tiny incisions. They have force capture sensors, which provide force feedback to the surgeon, putting the surgeon in contact with the tissue being manipulated.

Robotic-arm systems are also in place for interactive orthopedic system for minimally invasive orthopedic knee procedures like lateral knee resurfacing.

Robot hands are modeled after the human wrist, but offer an even greater range of motion than the human hand. They can do rapid and precise suturing, dissection and tissue manipulation.

Robotic 3-D ultrasound transducer can collect real time 3-D images at 10 to 15 times magnification from inside humans. With this, robots can accurately direct a needle on the end of the robotic arm to touch the tip of another needle within a blood vessel graft. The robot's needle is guided by a tiny transducer that collects the 3-D images, attached to a catheter commonly used in angioplasty procedures.

This 3-D technology allows robots to direct catheters inside synthetic blood vessels. Currently, cardiologists doing catheter-based procedures use fluoroscopy, which employs radiation, to guide their actions. Putting a 3-D ultrasound transducer on the end of the catheter could provide clearer images to the physician and greatly reduce the need for patients to be exposed to radiation. The technology also allows robots to perform a biopsy of a cyst.

Robots can be controlled remotely, allowing surgery on patients in dangerous situations or in remote locations, such as on the battlefield or in space.

Surgical robots can track a beating heart and compensate for its motion, allowing a surgeon to operate on it without having to stop the heart.

Other surgical robots are:

- Laparoscope-holding robot
- Image-guided localizer for neurosurgery
- Localizer for orthopedic surgery
- Automated endoscopic system for optimal positioning
- Surgical assistant system
- Computer-assisted surgical planning and robotics
- Advanced robotics for medical industry
- Trackless robotic courier

One day, sophisticated medical service robots can even conduct routine surgeries autonomously. Routine surgeries could get monotonous, but robots don't feel this same monotony.

Prescription Dispensing ATM

Pharmacist Robot ATMs dispense drugs to patients. They are found like ATM machines everywhere, and they dispense drugs after accessing online electronic medical records and prescriptions. They also advise patients of contraindications and other prescription related information. These robots reduce errors, and have instant labeling and automatic loading of medicines in ATM storage.

Nurse Robots

Medical robots can do nursing for patients in hospitals. Nurse robots can function independently or alongside surgeon robots. They can do hospital tasks like mopping up spillages, taking messages, and guiding visitors to hospital beds. They can distribute medicines and monitor the temperature of patients remotely with laser thermometers or thermal cameras. They clean wards, transport samples and specimens or move patients around a hospital.

These robots can sense how to get to the stress test lab, and they can push a patient in a wheelchair. They have a thermal imaging camera and they can observe the patient to see if they are too hot or cold, throughout the night when patients are asleep. They can coordinate things between themselves, such as deciding which one would be best-equipped to deal with patient fall from his bed, or to transport medicine.

Care Robots

Medical robots can do mundane tasks for the disabled, children, or elderly human beings who have limited mobility.

These robots can perform physical tasks like giving medications. They can even help the person in a way to communicate with friends, relatives, doctors, and so on.

Diagnostic toy robots are wearable and used for early diagnosis of neurodevelopmental disorders. Sensorized rattle toys are equipped with multiple inertial, magnetic, and tactile sensors for behavioral analysis of infants.

Mobile elder care robots are personal care robots with actionable situational awareness. They use multiple layers of sensors and sensor systems and apply sensor fusion technology.

Rehabilitation robots restore use of paralyzed limbs in brain-injured patients. The robotic arm braces can sense muscle signals that indicate deliberate intention to move; and then provides electronically-assisted movement.

Home assistance robots supply physical assistance to elderly patients who have difficulty moving or doing physical tasks around the house. They also assist people with cognitive difficulties due to Alzheimer's disease or other disorders.

Scheduling robots provide timely and repetitively verbal reminders for medicines, appointments, meals, and so on.

Diagnostic care robots can do evaluations and detect hearing loss, voice synthesis inadequacies, and other debilitating conditions.

Other care robots are robotic feeders, smart-powered wheelchairs, independent mobile robots, and socially assistive robots, robot spoons, robot arm feeding handicapped people, explorer all-terrain electric robotic assistant chair, assistive robot arm, assisted walking device, and a robot for carrying food trays to the aged and disabled.

Robotic Therapy

Robotic therapy helps reduce impairment and facilitate neural development of humans with various neurological problems like cerebral palsy, stroke, multiple sclerosis, Parkinson's disease, and spinal cord injury. In such cases the neurons in brains that survive the impairment can establish new synapses.

Therapy robots guide the limb as a patient tries to make a difficult movement of its limbs. This helps build missing neurological connections in brain and thus patients relearn how to move the limb on their own.

Such therapy is successful, but only after repeated movements, a task robots are very good at.

Robot Coaches

Parents are coached by baby robots. Baby robots look like a baby, with sensors and voice. They act and respond like a baby. This is given to the expectant parents to get real baby experience and what to expect with a newborn baby.

Dentists are coached by dental patient robots. The dental patient robot would look like a dental patient.

Robots can coach for welder training. These coach robots monitoring torch positions and torch motions and arc data while welding, providing in-helmet feedback to assist the welder to learn proper technique more quickly.

Golf coach robots can be golf companions both for practice as well as passing time. Golf coach robots can hold your golf club, feel your swing, and coach and help you practice the perfect swing.

Human looking robot coaches also teach in classrooms as math teachers and in labs as lab assistants. They can even conduct evaluations and give grades.

Conclusion

We have seen how intelligent environments have autonomous robots everywhere. These robots interact with humans and with each other to perform various services for them using sensors, control systems, manipulators, power supplies, and programming. These autonomous robots can be robot farmers, robot tractors, robot therapists, robots nurses, robot pharmacists, robot surgeons, and robot coaches.

Glossary

Advanced Encryption Standard instructions Advanced Encryption Standard (AES-NI) instructions are added to the architecture help accelerate data encryption and decryption, and improve performance.

Arrandale Intel's former processor code name of the Westmere-based mobile MCP (multi-chip package) in the Calpella platform (Intel® Core™ i7-620 processor or Intel® Core™ i5-520 processor paired with Intel® Mobile QM57 Express Chipset). Arrandale is comprised of a Hillel processor and the Ironlake GMCH (graphics and memory controller hub) in one package. Arrandale is the follow-on to the Nehalem-based Auburndale MCP.

Asymmetric Multiprocessing (AMP) AMP solutions partition hardware resources and run specific applications and operating systems in each partition. AMP is a good choice for CPU-bound applications that can be replicated across the cores without resource contention. Where applications are not well suited for parallelization, AMP can be a viable solution that benefits from the extra processing capabilities of Intel multi-core processors.

Boazman Intel's former code name for the Intel® 82567 LAN chip, a GbE single-port PHY manufactured on 90nm process technology and used as part of the Intel® Atom™ Processors N450, D410 and D510 with Intel® 82801HM I/O Controller platform, formerly code-named Luna Pier.

byte order Microprocessor architectures commonly use two different byte-ordering methods (little endian and big endian) to store the individual bytes of multi-byte data formats in memory. PowerPC is big endian and Intel architecture is little endian.

Byte ordering also affects structures and unions. Refer to the endianness section of the PowerPC† to Intel® Architecture Migration white paper for more information.

Calistoga Intel's former code name for the Mobile Intel® 945GSE Express Chipset.

Calpella Intel's former code name for the platform that combines the Intel® Core™ i7 Processor or Intel® Core™ i5 Processor (formerly Arrandale [Westmere 2C + Ironlake]) and Mobile Intel® QM57 Express Chipset (formerly Ibex Peak).

Cantiga Intel's former code name for the Mobile Intel® GM45, Intel® GS45, and Intel® GL40 Express family of chipsets.

Clarkdale Intel's former code name for the Intel® Core™ i5-660 processor, the Intel® Core™ i3-540 processor and the Intel® Pentium processor G6950 which can be paired with the Intel® 3450 Chipset or the Intel® Q57 Chipset on the Foxhollow or Piketon based platforms. It is the 2-core mainstream desktop variant of Westmere on LGA-1156. Clarkdale is a MCP (Multi-Chip Product) with a Westmere 2-core and Ironlake in a single package.

commercial temperature Intel products designed to operate in the temperature range: 0 to +70 degrees C.

data type conversions Intel architecture and PowerPC perform differently for some data type conversions, such as converting floating-point type to integer data types.

Diamondville Intel's former code name for the Intel® Atom™ Processor N270.

divide by zero For integer divide-by-zero, PowerPC simply returns zero. On Intel architecture, executing this operation is fatal. Code should always check the denominator for zero before executing the divide operation. There is no difference in operation between PowerPC and Intel architecture floating point divide-by-zero.

drivers and libraries If a PowerPC driver or library comes from a third-party vendor, check with the vendor for equivalent Intel architecture products. If the PowerPC driver is developed in-house, the low level initialization will need to be updated for Intel architecture. Open source versions of the driver may help guide the changes that are required. Intel architecture chipset datasheets contain information about registers that need to be programmed.

Intel® chipset drivers can be downloaded from the Intel Download Center. Navigate to Chipsets, then choose Embedded Chipsets. Intel® Embedded Graphics Drivers can be downloaded from Intel's Embedded Graphics Drivers Web site.

Eaglelake Intel's former code name for the Intel® Q45 Express Chipset.

ECC Error correcting code. An error detection and correction feature of certain DRAM memory.

Embedded At Intel embedded computing refers to using Intel's high performance platform solutions in nontraditional computing applications. In other words, embedded includes using Intel's processor and chipsets in computing systems other than desktop, notebook, and typical server computers. Examples of embedded computing systems include gaming (such as casino lottery, arcade, and amusement games); in-vehicle infotainment (such as onboard entertainment devices in cars); retail point of sale devices (such as intelligent cash registers and ATMs); industrial and home automation devices; energy management and control (such as smart grid technology); military, aerospace and government computing; telecommunications; medical (such as imaging, and patient monitoring and portable devices).

embedded flexible design (Intel® Embedded Flexible Design) Intel® Embedded Flexible Design enables scalability for the first time on the Intel® Atom™ processors N450, D410 and D510 with Intel® 82801HM I/O Controller.

embedded graphics Intel® Embedded Graphics Drivers (IEGD) specifically target the needs of embedded platform developers. With a flexible architecture, extending to the video BIOS, and a new UEFI video driver, this driver set speeds time-to-market by enabling you to customize configurations in-house.

embedded Menlow XL The Intel® Atom™ processor Z5xx series is available in small form factor (13x14mm package) and large form factor (22x22mm package) versions. The Intel® System Controller Hub US15W is similarly available in small form factor (22x22mm package) and large form factor (37.5x37.5mm package) versions. Embedded Menlow XL (eMenlow XL) is the code name for the validated Intel platform that combines the large form factor versions of the Intel Atom Processor Z5xx Series (formerly code-named Silverthorne XL) and the Intel System Controller Hub (formerly code-named Poulsbo XL).

Embedded remote labs Users can establish a secure remote connection to physical platform hardware enabling test, evaluation and optimization of Intel® architecture.

embedded roadmap The embedded Intel roadmap includes product platforms for embedded design that have long life support (7 years). There are three main roadmap vectors: performance, scalability and low power.

eMenlow (embedded Menlow) eMenlow is the former code name for validated Intel platform that combines the Intel® Atom Processor Z5xx Series (formerly code-named Silverthorne) with the Intel® System Controller Hub (formerly code-named Poulsbo).

Endianness Endianness describes how multi-byte data is represented by a computer system and is dictated by the CPU architecture of the system.

Enhanced Intel® Speedstep® Technology (EIST) Enhanced Intel® SpeedStep® Technology and demand-based switching allows the processor performance and power consumption levels to be modified while a system is functioning by separately adjusting processor voltage and core frequency. This results in decreased average power consumption and decreased average heat production while meeting performance requirements.

EP (as in Nehalem-EP) An Intel abbreviation for efficient performance.

execute disable bit Execute disable bit is a hardware-based security feature that can reduce exposure to viruses and malicious code attacks and prevent harmful software from executing and propagating on the server or networks.

Extensible Firmware Interface (EFI) Intel promotes Extensible Firmware Interface (EFI) as a C language based modular firmware alternative to traditional BIOS. The EFI specification defines a model for the interface between operating systems and platform firmware. The interface consists of data tables that contain platform-related information, plus boot and runtime service calls that are available to the operating system and its loader. Together, these provide a standard environment for booting an operating system and running pre-boot applications.

The Unified EFI (UEFI) Forum was formed to manage and promote the EFI specification, and EFI was renamed to UEFI. Visit the UEFI Web site for more information.

Fort Sumter Intel's former code name for the customer reference board based on the Intel® Core™ i7 Processor or Intel® Core™ i5 Processor and Mobile Intel® QM57 Express Chipset; supports ECC.

Foxhollow Intel's former code name for the platform that combines the Intel® Core™ i5 Processor or Intel® Core™ i3 Processor or Intel® Pentium® or Intel® Xeon® Processor and Intel® 3450 Chipset. A Foxhollow platform system contains either a Lynnfield (Nehalem 4C) or Clarkdale (Westmere 2C + Ironlake) processor and Ibex Peak chipset.

high-definition multimedia interface A digital interface for transmitting uncompressed video and audio data.

Ibex Peak Intel's former code name for a PCH used on Nehalem mobile and desktop platforms. It is a successor of ICH10, which includes the Intel® 5 series chipsets and Intel® 3400 series chipsets.

industrial (or extended) temperature Intel products designed to operate in the temperature range: -40 to +85 degrees C.

input/output controller 82801HM (Intel® 82801 HM I/O Controller) The Intel® 82801 HM I/O controller provides rich I/O capabilities and flexibility with high-bandwidth interfaces such as PCI Express*, PCI, Serial ATA, and Hi-Speed USB 2.0. It includes a single channel for DDR2 system memory and an Intel® High Definition Audio interface.

input/output controller ICH8M Intel's former name for the Intel® 82801HM I/O controller used on the Intel® Atom™ processors N450, D410 and D510 with Intel® 82801HM I/O Controller platform, formerly code-named Luna Pier.

instructions PowerPC and Intel architecture instructions differ. For some instructions there is no one-to-one equivalent. Refer to the assembly code section of the PowerPC to Intel Architecture Migration white paper for the appropriate Intel® Software Developer Manuals, instruction set information and tools that may assist the assembly code migration.

Intel® Active Management Technology (Intel AMT) Intel® AMT comprises a set of hardware-based remote management and maintenance capabilities that enable IT professionals to query, fix, and protect networked embedded devices, even when they are powered off, not responding or have software issues. A part of Intel® vPro™ technology, Intel AMT helps perform remote asset tracking and checks the presence of management agents. Devices can be remotely turned on/off to reduce energy consumption during non-peak operating times.

Intel® Atom™ processors The Intel® Atom™ processor is Intel's smallest processor, built with the world's smallest transistors and manufactured on Intel's industry-leading 45nm high-k metal gate technology.

Intel® Atom™ Processor D410 (Intel® Atom™ D410 desktop processor for embedded computing) The single-core Intel® Atom™ processor N410, based on Intel® 45nm process technology, features integrated graphics and memory controllers for robust performance. Intel® Embedded Flexible Design enables scalability for the first time on Intel Atom processors.

Intel® Atom™ Processor N450 (Intel® Atom™ N450 mobile processors for embedded computing) Based on Intel® 45nm process technology, the Intel® Atom™ processor N450 features single-core processing and Intel® Enhanced Deeper Sleep (C4/C4E) which reduces power consumption while the processor is idle.

Intel® Atom™ Processor D510 (Intel® Atom™ D510 desktop processor for embedded computing) Based on Intel® 45nm process technology, the Intel® Atom™ processor N510 features dual-core processing which performs full parallel execution of multiple software threads to enable higher levels of performance over the previous-generation Intel® Atom™ processor N270.

Intel® Celeron® processors Intel® Celeron® processors deliver exceptional value and reliability for basic computing requirements.

Intel® Celeron® M processors The Intel® Celeron® M processors provide a balanced level of mobile-optimized processor technology, good performance, and exceptional value for basic computing requirements.

Intel® Core™ microarchitecture Intel® Core™ microarchitecture is the foundation for new Intel® architecture-based desktop, mobile, and mainstream server multi-core processors.

Intel® Core™2 processors Intel® Core™2 processors include Intel's 64-bit family of single core, dual core (Core™2 Duo) and quad core (Core™2 Quad) processors based on Intel® Core™ microarchitecture.

Intel® Core™2 Duo processors Based on Intel® Core™ microarchitecture, the Intel® Core™2 Duo processor family combines two independent processor cores in one physical package. The processors run at the same frequency and share up to 6 MB of L2 cache and up to 1333 MHz front side bus for truly parallel computing.

Intel® Core™2 Quad processors Based on Intel® Core™ microarchitecture, the Intel® Core™2 Quad processor family combines four processing cores, up to 12 MB of shared L2 cache and 1333 MHz front side bus to deliver amazing performance and power efficiency.

Intel® Core™ i3 desktop processors for embedded computing Based on Intel® 32nm process technology, the Intel® Core™ i3-540 processor features dual-core processing and Intel® Hyper-Threading Technology (Intel® HT Technology), which enables simultaneous multi-threading to help boost performance for parallel, multi-threaded applications. The complete product line is labeled under the generic Intel® Core™ processor brand, which includes Intel® Core™ i3 Processor and Intel® Q57 Chipset code name Piketon platform and Intel® Core™ i3 Processor and Intel® 3450 Chipset formerly code named Foxhollow platform.

Intel® Core™ i5 desktop processors for embedded computing In dual-core (32nm) and quad-core (45nm) implementations, Intel® Core™ i5 desktop processors feature Intel® Turbo Boost Technology that can automatically allocate processing power where it is needed. They are designed to meet the needs of performance-intensive embedded applications. The complete product line is labeled under the generic Intel® Core™ processor brand, which includes Intel® Core™ i5 Processor and Intel® Q57 Chipset code name Piketon platform.

Intel® Core™ i5 mobile processors for embedded computing Based on 32nm process technology, dual-core Intel® Core™ i5 processors feature intelligent performance, power efficiency, integrated graphics, and error correcting code (ECC) memory on industry-standard x86 architecture. The complete product line is labeled under the generic Intel® Core™ processor brand, which includes Intel® Core™ i5 Processor and Mobile Intel® QM57 Express Chipset formerly code named Calpella platform and Intel® Core™ i5 Processor and Intel® 3450 Chipset formerly code named Foxhollow platform.

Intel® Core™ i7 desktop processors for embedded computing Based on Intel® 45nm process technology, the Intel® Core i7 processor features quad-core processing and intelligent performance capabilities, such as Intel® Turbo Boost Technology and Intel® Hyper-Threading Technology (Intel® HT Technology) for demanding embedded applications. The complete product line is labeled under the generic Intel® Core™ processor brand, which includes Intel® Core™ i7 Processor and Intel® Q57 Chipset code name Piketon platform.

Intel® Core™ i7 mobile processors for embedded computing Based on 32nm process technology, dual-core Intel® Core™ i7 processors feature intelligent performance, power efficiency, integrated graphics, and error correcting code (ECC) memory on industry-standard x86 architecture. The complete product line is labeled under the generic Intel® Core™ processor brand, which includes Intel® Core™ i7 Processor and Mobile Intel® QM57 Express Chipset formerly code named Calpella platform.

Intel® Enhanced Deeper Sleep (C4/C4E) Deep sleep (C3) and deeper sleep (C4) are terms used in the power management of mobile platforms, improving battery life by putting the CPU to "sleep" when not in use. C3 and C4 refer to ACPI power management states.

Intel® EP80579 Integrated Processors Based on Intel architecture, the Intel® EP80579 Integrated Processor product line is the first in a series of breakthrough system on-a-chip (SOC) processors, delivering excellent performance-per-watt for small form factor designs.

Intel® firmware hub The Intel® firmware hub includes a 5-signal communication interface used to control the operation of the device in a system environment. Buffers for this interface are designed to be PCI-compliant.

Intel® High-Definition Audio Intel® High-Definition Audio is Intel's next-generation architecture for implementing audio, modem and communications functionality. As an integrated controller, it supports multimedia applications and differentiation through the use of a variety of third-party audio codecs.

Intel® Hyper-Threading Technology (Intel HT Technology) Intel Hyper-Threading Technology enables thread-level parallelism on each processor resulting in more efficient use of processor resources–higher processing throughput–and improved performance on today's multithreaded software. Intel HT Technology requires a computer system with an Intel® processor supporting Intel HT Technology and an Intel HT Technology-enabled chipset, BIOS, and operating system.

Intel® Intelligent Power Technology Intel® Intelligent Power Technology reduces idle power consumption through architectural improvements such as integrated power gates and automated low-power states.

Intel® I/O Acceleration Technology Intel® I/O Acceleration Technology (Intel® I/OAT), a component of Intel® Virtualization Technology for Connectivity, improves data flow across the platform to enhance system performance. The Intel® I/OAT implements system wide enhancements ensure that the data gets to and from applications consistently faster and with greater reliability.

Intel® Multi-Core Technology By incorporating multiple processor execution cores in a single package, Intel® Multi-Core Technology delivers full parallel execution of multiple software threads. This enables higher levels of performance while using same power typically required by higher frequency single core processor. Intel Multi-Core Technology along with Intel® Virtualization Technology enables platform consolidation, and increase system utilization and performance.

Intel® power management technologies Intel power management technologies enable systems to strike the right balance between computing performance needs and power consumption by automatically adjusting the power state to use only the energy required by the workload. The Intel power technologies comprises of Enhanced Intel® SpeedStep® Technology, Intel® Turbo Boost Technology and Dynamic FSB frequency switching mechanism.

Intel® QuickAssist Technology Intel® QuickAssist Technology is a comprehensive initiative to optimize the use and deployment of accelerators on Intel® architecture platforms.

Intel® Streaming SIMD Extensions 2 (Intel SSE2) Intel® Streaming SIMD Extensions (SSE) 2 enables software to accelerate data processing in specific areas, such as complex arithmetic and video decoding, by extending MMX instructions to operate on XMM registers.

Intel® Streaming SIMD Extensions 3 (Intel SSE3) Intel® SSE3, an extension of SSE2, enables software to accelerate data processing by working horizontally in a register, as opposed to the more or less strictly vertical operation of all previous SSE instructions.

Intel® Supplemental Streaming SIMD Extensions 3 (Intel SSSE3) Intel® SSE3, an extension of SSE3, contains 16 new discrete instructions (that can act on 64-bit MMX or 128-bit XMM registers) over SSE3, enabling software to accelerate data processing.

Intel® Trusted Execution Technology Intel® Trusted Execution Technology (Intel® TXT), formerly code-named LaGrande Technology, is a versatile set of hardware extensions to Intel® processors and chipsets that enhance the digital office platform with security capabilities such as measured launch and protected execution.

Intel® Turbo Boost Technology Intel® Turbo Boost Technology automatically allows processor cores to run faster than the base operating frequency if it's operating below power, current, and temperature specification limits.

Intel® Virtualization Technology (Intel® VT) The virtualization technology provides maximum system utilization by consolidating multiple environments into a single server or PC. Hardware–based Intel® Virtualization Technology improves the fundamental flexibility and robustness of traditional software–based virtualization solutions by accelerating key functions of the virtualized platform.

Intel® Virtualization Technology for Connectivity (Intel® VT-C) Intel® Virtualization Technology for Connectivity is collection of I/O virtualization technologies that improves overall system performance by improving communication between host CPU and I/O devices within the virtual server. This enables a lowering of CPU utilization, a reduction of system latency and improved networking and I/O throughput.

Intel® Virtualization Technology for Directed I/O (Intel® VT-d) Intel® Virtualization Technology for Directed I/O (VT-d) extends Intel's Virtualization Technology (VT) roadmap by providing hardware assists for virtualization solutions. VT-d adds support for I/O-device virtualization to help end users improve security and reliability systems and improve performance of I/O devices in a virtualized environment.

Intel® vPro™ technology Intel® vPro™ technology enables IT personnel to take advantage of hardware-assisted security and manageability capabilities that enhance their ability to maintain, manage, and protect computing systems.

local area network controller (LAN) 82567 Based on 90nm process technology, the Intel® 82567 controller is a GbE Single-Port PHY that features a small footprint 10/100/1000 design.

low power Low power is an embedded Intel roadmap vector that focuses on applications that have either tight thermal constraints or require smaller form factors. These platforms are generally mobile PC class products (mobile/notebook/netbook), including the newest ultra low power Intel Atom processor family.

Luna Pier Intel's former code name for the Intel® Atom™ processors N450, D410 and D510 with Intel® 82801HM I/O Controller platform.

Lynnfield Intel's former code name of a Nehalem based quad-core desktop processor, and initially released as the Intel® Core™ i5-750, Core™ i7-860, and Core™ i7-870 processors as well as the Xeon X3400 processor series. It is designed for the Foxhollow and Piketon platforms with the Ibex Peak chipset. Lynnfield contains the Nehalem Core and Uncore elements, and a reduced version of the Thurley platform MCH (Tylersburg) in the same package (called the IIO). The QuickPath link between the Core/Uncore elements and the IIO is also internal.

McCreary Intel's former code name for validated Intel platform that combines Intel® Core™2 Quad Processor Q9400 (formerly code-named Yorkfield) or Intel® Core™2 Duo Processor E8400 (formerly code-named Wolfdale) with Intel® Q45 Express Chipset (formerly code-named Eaglelake).

Montevina Intel's former code name for validated Intel platform that combines Intel® Core™2 Duo, Intel® Celeron® and Intel® Celeron® M processors (formerly code-named Penryn family) with Mobile Intel® GM45, Intel® GS45, and Intel® GL40 Express Chipset (formerly code-named Cantiga family).

Moon Creek customer reference board (CRB) Intel's name for the Intel® Atom™ processors N450, D410 and D510 with Intel® 82801HM I/O Controller customer reference board.

Moore's law First articulated by Intel co-founder Gordon Moore, Moore's law states that the number of transistors on a chip will double about every two years.

Motherboard A printed circuit board (PCB) used to support and electrically interconnect electronic devices such as the processor, chipset, memory, and I/O devices. In embedded computing the motherboard is generally the primary PCB, which may also include ancillary PCB's (daughter-boards, such as Wi-Fi and mezzanines).

Navy Pier Intel's former code name for validated Intel platform that combines Intel® Atom™ Processor N270 (formerly code-named Diamondville) and Mobile Intel® 945GSE Express Chipset (formerly code-named Calistoga).

Nehalem-EP Intel's former code name for the Intel® Xeon® Processor 5500 series.

Palomar Intel's former code name for the customer reference board based on the Intel® Core™ i5 or Intel® Core™ i3 or Intel® Pentium® or Intel® Xeon® Processors and Intel® 3450 Chipset.

Penryn Intel's former code name for Intel® Core™2 Duo T9400/SL9400/SU9300/SP9300, Intel® Celeron® and Intel® Celeron® M ULV 722 processors.

Pentium® (Intel® Pentium® processors) Intel® Pentium® processors include a family of Intel® processors that delivers great performance, low power enhancements and multitasking for everyday computing.

Pentium M (Intel® Pentium® M processors) Intel® Pentium® M processors are based on Intel's initial mobile processing technology designed specifically for notebooks to deliver great mobile performance and low power enhancements.

Performance Performance is an embedded Intel roadmap vector that supports processors and chipsets focused on high compute performance, dual processor, data integrity features, large memory footprint and high I/O throughput. It includes many of the enterprise and server platforms as well as mobile processors paired with server class chipsets.

Piketon Intel's former codename for the platform based on the Intel® Core™ i7 Processor or Intel® Core™ i5 Processor or Intel® Core™ i3 Processor or Intel® Pentium® Processor and Intel® Q57 Chipset. A Piketon platform system contains either a Lynnfield (Nehalem 4C) or Clarkdale (Westmere 2C + Ironlake) processor and Ibex Peak chipset.

Pineview-D (Pineview Desktop) Intel's former code name for the Intel® Atom™ processor D410 or Intel® Atom™ processor N510.

Pineview-M (or Pineview Mobile) Intel's former code name for the Intel® Atom™ N450 processor.

Platform A platform is a validated combination of an Intel processor with an Intel® chipset.

Poulsbo Intel's former code name for the Intel® System Controller Hub.

processor number Once you have decided on the processor brand family that is right for your design, Intel processor numbers allow you to quickly differentiate among processors within that product family. The numbers are based on a variety of features that may include the processor's underlying architecture, cache, front side bus (FSB), clock speed, power and other Intel® technologies.

Real-time operating system An real-time operating system supports deterministic performance, which can be defined as a guaranteed response within a set period of time. Real-time operating systems are often used in embedded systems to achieve optimized performance, enabled by low interrupt latency and rapid context switching.

Red Fort Intel's former code name for the customer reference board based on the non-ECC versions of the Intel® Core™ i7 Processor or Intel® Core™ i5 Processor and Mobile Intel® QM57 Express Chipset.

Registration The Basic User level provides open access to public content on the site. registering as a basic user lets you share ideas and insights and collaborate with other members of the Intel® embedded community.

The Privileged User level provides Basic User benefits plus password-protected access to Intel confidential technical content such as schematic files, simulation models, technical trainings, electronic support, free hardware test tools, and much more.

scalability Scalability is an embedded Intel roadmap vector that focuses on applications that can benefit from the flexibility of using multiple processors in a single board design. Products scale vertically to offer multiple price and performance options and horizontally from one processor generation to the next. These platforms are generally desktop PC class products.

Silverthorne Intel's former code name for the Intel® Atom™ Processor Z5xx Series.

64-bit Intel® 64 architecture delivers 64-bit computing on server, workstation, desktop and mobile platforms when combined with supporting software. Intel 64 architecture improves performance by allowing systems to address more than 4 GB of both virtual and physical memory. Intel 64 provides support for 64-bit flat virtual address space, 64-bit pointers, 64-bit wide general purpose registers, 64-bit integer support and up to one terabyte (TB) of platform address space.

SOC Abbreviation for system-on-a-chip.

software development tools Understanding the needs and availability of tools for the new platform is important when investigating the requirements of the port. Keep in mind that software development tools, as with all software applications, have system requirements. The tool must support the target processor and operating system.

SpeedStep® Technology The conventional Intel® SpeedStep® Technology switches both voltage and frequency in tandem between high and low levels in response to processor load.

Step-by-Step Step-by-Step is a 4-step design guide on the Intel® Embedded Design Center (Intel® EDC) that enables embedded developers to Explore, Evaluate, Design and Build embedded applications.

symmetric multiprocessing (SMP) SMP operating systems treat all cores as equals and distribute the workload/processing to the available cores. An SMP design is an efficient way to take advantage of multi-core hardware. It can be written to scale performance automatically as the number of processing cores increases. More operating systems are now providing SMP, including embedded RTOSs, but SMP requires code to be architected to take advantage of parallelization with multiple CPUs. For situations where applications are not well suited for parallelization, asymmetric multiprocessing (AMP) could be a better solution to benefit from the extra processing capabilities of multi-core hardware. RTOS vendors that provide real-time SMP support for IA include:

system initialization firmware Every embedded Intel architecture design must include a firmware stack that initializes CPU cores, memory, IO, peripherals and often graphics. It may also include respective diagnostic routines. In any case, the initialization gets the system to a point where the operating system can load. PowerPC systems use home-grown boot loaders, but achieving system initialization on Intel architecture is easy for situations where developing a home-grown boot loader is less desirable.

structures and unions The fields in a structure can be sensitive to the defined order. Structures must either be properly ordered or directly accessed by the field name.

thermal design power The power dissipation target for thermal solution design, based on a realistic worst-case application running at the maximum component temperature. Note: thermal design power is not maximum power.

Tolapai Former code name for the Intel® EP80579 Integrated Processor, a system-on-a-chip (SOC).

Tylersburg Intel's former code name for the Intel® 5520 Chipset.

Tylersburg-EP Intel's former code name for the platform based on the Intel® Xeon® Processor 5500 Series and the Intel® 5520 Chipset.

vector oriented instructions PowerPC uses AltiVec† instructions. Intel architecture uses streaming SIMD extensions (SSE). Refer to the vector oriented code section of PowerPC† to Intel® Architecture Migration white paper for details about migrating AltiVec to SSE instructions.

Westmere Formerly referred to as Nehalem-C, is the code name of a processor. It is the P1268 (32 nm) compaction of Nehalem. Gulftown is high-end server version on LGA-1366. Clarkdale is the mainstream version on LGA-1156. Arrandale is the mobile version.

Wolfdale Intel's former code name for the Intel® Core™2 Duo Processor E8400.

Yorkfield Intel's former code name for the Intel® Core™2 Quad Processor Q9400.

www.ingramcontent.com/pod-product-compliance
Lightning Source LLC
Chambersburg PA
CBHW080410060326

40689CB00019B/4191